*THE NEGRO CHURCH
IN AMERICA*

---

*THE BLACK CHURCH
SINCE FRAZIER*

E. FRANKLIN FRAZIER

The Negro Church in America

The Black Church Since Frazier

C. ERIC LINCOLN

Schocken Books • New York

The Negro Church in America, by E. Franklin Frazier (1894–1962), was first published in the United States in 1964 and has since seen nine printings in its hardcover and paperback editions. Deeming the significant events of the 1960s and 1970s important matter for appraisal in the light of Frazier's work, the publishers commissioned C. Eric Lincoln to write a second small volume, *The Black Church Since Frazier.* Accordingly, this new edition is published as two volumes in one, the text of each individual work retaining its own integrity and identity. In resetting *The Negro Church in America* for this edition, minor changes in spelling and punctuation have been made to conform with American usage.

The Black Church Since Frazier originated as The James Gray Lectures given at Duke University in 1970.

Library of Congress Catalog Card Number 72-96201

ISBN 0-8052-0387-7

Manufactured in the United States of America
B   9   8   7   6

CONTENTS

CONTENTS

THE NEGRO CHURCH
IN AMERICA

E. FRANKLIN FRAZIER

PREFACE

THE sudden and most untimely death of Franklin Frazier has compelled us to accept the necessity to publish this volume as a tribute to his memory. It will be found to be a valuable addition to his works, dealing with a subject of great intrinsic importance, written (as was always the case with Professor Frazier's books) with sympathy and insight, and in the most lucid and attractive prose. The volume starts with an appreciation of his achievements by his colleague and friend, Professor Everett Hughes. All who were privileged to know Professor Frazier will be grateful to Professor Hughes for his tribute, and will appreciate its warmth.

T. S. SIMEY

E. FRANKLIN FRAZIER:
A MEMOIR BY
EVERETT C. HUGHES

FRANKLIN FRAZIER, by a sort of genius for essentials, devoted his career mainly to the study of two American institutions, the Negro family and the Negro church. Barred from full and equal participation in any of the public institutions of the country and not permitted to develop their own in most realms of life, American Negroes were "free"—in an ironic sense—to develop their own family and religious life. By American caste rule, no person of any degree of known Negro ancestry can be "kin" to any person supposedly of no such ancestry. Negro Americans had to make their own family institutions. White Americans, who became white because they had black slaves, having made Christians of their field hands, did not want to commune with them from the same cup. Hence at birth, confirmation, communion, marriage, death, and all the great turning points and festivals, Negro and white were alien to each other. The separation was not quite reciprocal. Negroes were often spectators, and more, of the intimate life of whites, while the whites—although they had no shame about intruding—saw little of the intimate life of Negroes. Religion and family became foci of Negro life in a special degree.

But the story of the American Negro family and church has been told by Frazier himself. Let me talk of the man. He studied with Robert E. Park at the University of Chicago.

Now Park, although intensely interested in the social attitudes of which his colleague William I. Thomas wrote so much, insisted that the psychology of race, or of anything else, be studied in whole ecological and social settings. He set us, his students, to studying the various kinds of economic, political, and social arrangements which grew up where races and nations met and especially where one had great power over another. I did not know Frazier before he had studied with Park, but certainly the toughness and subtlety of Park's approach came naturally to him. He became our toughest student of race relations; tough on well-meaning whites who tried to escape full responsibility for American racial injustice by inviting nice Negroes to dinner to prove they had no prejudice; tough on all who let condescension creep into their talk or actions; but toughest of all on those American Negroes who used segregation as a wall behind which to hide in a whining, comfortable, snobbish mediocrity. *Black Bourgeoisie*, in which he castigated his fellows, may, as a social and political tract, be Frazier's greatest contribution. Americans of any hue, if they read it well, will wince as they feel his touch in their moral wounds. Nor is *Black Bourgeoisie* only incidentally about *Negro* Americans.

Race and Culture Contacts in the Modern World might also be considered Frazier's best work. But that would be like making a Beethoven symphony compete with a quartet. It is of another *genre*. In it Frazier gives to the academic world the essence of Robert E. Park's system of analysis of racial relations. To one who knew both men well, this book is an organic blend of the thoughts of the two. It is no belittling of Frazier to say that in this book he writes as a disciple; a disciple, well-ripened, who feels no need to deny his debt.

Fortunately Frazier has left us a full sample of his work and thought, from the intimacy of *The Negro Family in the United States*, warmth and liveliness of *The Negro Church in America*, and the lashing criticism of *Black Bourgeoisie*, to the historic sweep of *The Negro in the United States* and the world-wide perspective of *Race and Culture in the Modern World*. But he has not left on paper the warm humanity of a man who felt in every fiber the human comedy and the human tragedy—which are one—visited in special degree on Americans of some Negro ancestry.

INTRODUCTION

In 1953, I had the unexpected honor to be invited to give the Frazer Lecture in Social Anthropology at the University of Liverpool. At the time I was serving as the Chief of the Division of the Applied Social Sciences in the Department of Social Sciences of UNESCO in Paris. The choice of a subject for the Frazer Lecture did not present any special difficulty since it would most appropriately be in the field of religion and I had given some attention to religion in my studies of the American Negro. The main difficulty arose from the fact that I was far from the sources of information which were necessary to treat the subject adequately. The paper which I read on the occasion of the lecture, entitled "The Evolution of Religion Among American Negroes," presented in barest outlines the thesis of this book. It had been my hope, at the time, that when I returned to the United States I would be able to expand the original lecture on the basis of the materials which I had in my files. But it turned out that previously contracted writing obligations and teaching requirements delayed my expanding the lecture for publication. One compensating feature of the delay has been that it enabled me to give more reflection to the subject as well as to consult new sources of information. However, the basic thesis of the lecture has not been changed, namely, that the changes in the religious life of the Negro in the United States can be understood only in terms of the social organization and social disorganization of Negro life. The use of the term "evolution" in the original title was perhaps unfortunate because it might have suggested that the lecture was concerned with stages in the development of religion among Negroes. This study, as now presented, is therefore concerned with the broad problem of the relation of religion to social structure or, more specifically, the role of religion in the social organization of Negro life in the United States.

There are a number of studies which have dealt with the Negro church and Negro religion in a general way, the most important among them being W. E. B. DuBois, *The Negro Church;* Carter G. Woodson, *The History of the Negro Church;* and Benjamin E. Mays and Joseph W. Nicholson, *The Negro's Church.* To this number should be added Arthur H. Fauset's *Black Gods of the Metropolis*, which is the most valuable study of the new Negro cults in the city, and the descriptive material contained in the chapters dealing with religion in St. Clair Drake and Horace R. Cayton, *Black Metropolis.*

Grateful acknowledgment is due to the Council, Senate, and Faculty of Arts of the University of Liverpool for the invitation to give the Frazer Lecture and to Professor T. S. Simey both for the invitation and for his patience in waiting for the manuscript. A mere expression of gratitude is a small acknowledgment of my indebtedness to Mrs. Dorothy B. Porter of the Moorland Foundation Library, Howard University, whose wide knowledge of sources is indispensable to anyone working in the field of the Negro. Thanks are also due to Mrs. Louise C. Smith and Mrs. Willia P. Lewis for typing the manuscript under extremely difficult conditions. Finally, appreciation is due to my wife, whose father was a Baptist minister who built a school and established several churches, was a leader in fraternal organizations, and was once active in politics, for her intimate knowledge of the Negro church which was a part of her family heritage.

E. FRANKLIN FRAZIER

Washington, D.C.

1

THE RELIGION
OF THE SLAVES

The Break with the African Background

IN studying any phase of the character and the development
of the social and cultural life of the Negro in the United
States, one must recognize from the beginning that because
of the manner in which the Negroes were captured in Africa
and enslaved, they were practically stripped of their social
heritage.[1] Although the area in West Africa from which the
majority of the slaves were drawn exhibits a high degree of
cultural homogeneity, the capture of many of the slaves in
intertribal wars and their selection for the slave markets
tended to reduce to a minimum the possibility of the reten-
tion and the transmission of African culture. The slaves
captured in the intertribal wars were generally males and
those selected for the slave markets on the African coasts were
the young and the most vigorous. This was all in accordance
with the demands of the slave markets in the New World.
One can get some notion of this selective process from the
fact that it was not until 1840 that the number of females
equalled the number of males in the slave population of the
United States.[2] Young males, it will be readily agreed, are
poor bearers of the cultural heritage of a people.

But the manner in which the slaves were held for the slave
ships that transported them to the New World also had an
important influence upon the transmission of the African
social heritage to the new environment. They were held in

baracoons, a euphemistic term for concentration camps at the time, where the slaves without any regard for sex or family and tribal affiliations were kept until some slaver came along to buy a cargo for the markets of the New World. This period of dehumanization was followed by the "middle passage," the voyage across the Atlantic Ocean to the slave markets of the West Indies and finally the indigo, tobacco, and cotton plantations of what was to become later the United States. During the "middle passage," the Negroes were packed spoon-fashion in the slave ships, where no regard was shown for sex or age differences, not to mention such matters as clan and tribal differences. In fact, no regard was shown for such elementary social, or shall I say human, considerations as family ties.

In the New World the process by which the Negro was stripped of his social heritage and thereby, in a sense, dehumanized was completed.[3] There was first the size of the plantation, which had a significant influence upon the extent and nature of the contacts between the slaves and the whites. On the large sugar and cotton plantations in the Southern States there was, as in Brazil and the West Indies, little contact between whites and the Negro slaves. Under such conditions there was some opportunity for the slaves to undertake to re-establish their old ways. As a matter of fact, however, the majority of slaves in the United States were on small farms and small plantations. In some of the upland cotton regions of Alabama, Mississippi, Louisiana, and Arkansas the median number of slaves per holding did not reach twenty; while in regions of general agriculture based mainly upon slave labor in Kentucky, Maryland, Missouri, North Carolina, South Carolina, and Tennessee the median number of slave holdings was even smaller.[4]

Then slaves freshly imported from Africa were usually "broken in" to the plantation régime. According to the descriptions given by a traveler in Louisiana, the new slaves were only "gradually accustomed to work. They are made to bathe often, to take long walks from time to time, and especially to dance; they are distributed in small numbers among old slaves in order to dispose them better to acquire their habits."[5] Apparently from all reports, these new slaves with their African ways were subjected to the disdain, if not hostility, of Negroes who had become accommodated to the plantation régime and had acquired the ways of their new environment.

Of what did accommodation to their new environment consist? It was necessary to acquire some knowledge of the language of whites for communication. Any attempt on the part of the slaves to preserve or use their native language was discouraged or prohibited. They were set to tasks in order to acquire the necessary skills for the production of cotton or sugar cane. On the small farms very often the slaves worked in the fields with their white owners. On the larger plantations they were under the strict discipline of the overseers, who not only supervised their work but who also in the interest of security maintained a strict surveillance over all their activities. It was a general rule that there could be no assembly of five or more slaves without the presence of a white man. This applied especially to their gathering for religious purposes. Later we shall see how the slaves were soon introduced into the religious life of their white masters. All of this tended to bring about as completely as possible a loss of the Negro's African cultural heritage.

The Loss of Social Cohesion

It is evident, then, that the manner in which Negroes were captured and enslaved and inducted into the plantation régime tended to loosen all social bonds among them and to destroy the traditional basis of social cohesion. In addition, the organization of labor and the system of social control and discipline on the plantation both tended to prevent the development of social cohesion either on the basis of whatever remnants of African culture might have survived or on the basis of the Negroes' role in the plantation economy. Although the Negroes were organized in work gangs, labor lost its traditional African meaning as a cooperative undertaking with communal significance. In fact, there was hardly a community among the slaves despite the fact that on the larger plantations there were slave quarters. These slave quarters were always under the surveillance of the overseer. On the smaller plantations which included, as we have seen, the majority of the plantations, the association between master and slave became the basis of a new type of social cohesion. However, this will be discussed in the next section.

Let us consider next a factor of equal if not greater importance in the plantation régime that tended to destroy all social cohesion among the slaves. I refer to the mobility of the slave population which resulted from the fact that the plantation in the Southern States was a commercial form of agriculture requiring the buying and selling of slaves. There has been much controversy about the slave trade because of its dehumanizing nature. Curiously enough, southern apologists for slavery deny, on the one hand, that there was a domestic slave trade while, on the other hand, they insist that slave traders were despised and were regarded as outcasts in southern society.[6] There were defenders, however, of the system who frankly acknowledged that slave-trading was indispensable to the slave system. The Charleston *Mercury,* for example, stated that "Slaves . . . are as much and as frequently articles of commerce as the sugar and molasses which they produce."[7] This opinion has been confirmed by the study of the practice during slavery.[8] The slave trade, we may conclude, was one of the important factors that tended toward the atomization and dehumanizing of the slaves.

The possibility of establishing some basis for social cohesion was further reduced because of the difficulty of communication among the slaves. If by chance slaves who spoke the same African language were thrown together, it was the policy on the part of the masters to separate them. In any case it was necessary for the operation of the plantation that the slaves should learn the language of their masters and communication among slaves themselves was generally carried on in English. In recent years a study has revealed that among the relatively isolated Negroes on the Sea Islands along the coast of South Carolina and Georgia, many African words have been preserved in the Negro dialect known as Gullah.[9] But the very social isolation of these Negroes is an indication of the exceptional situation in which some remnants of African languages were preserved in the American environment. It is important to note that, according to the author of this study, the use of African modes of English speech and African speech survivals were used only within the family group. This brings us to the most important aspect of the loss of social cohesion among the Negroes as the result of enslavement.

The enslavement of the Negro not only destroyed the traditional African system of kinship and other forms of organized social life but it made insecure and precarious the most elementary form of social life which tended to sprout anew, so to speak, on American soil—the family. There was, of course, no legal marriage and the relation of the husband and father to his wife and children was a temporary relationship dependent upon the will of the white masters and the exigencies of the plantation régime.[10] Although it was necessary to show some regard for the biological tie between slave mother and her offspring, even this relationship was not always respected by the masters. Nevertheless, under the most favorable conditions of slavery as, for example, among the privileged skilled artisans and the favored house servants, some stability in family relations and a feeling of solidarity among the members of the slave households did develop. This, in fact, represented the maximum social cohesion that was permitted to exist among the transplanted Negroes.

There have been some scholars who have claimed that social cohesion among the slaves was not destroyed to the extent to which it is presented here. For example, DuBois evidently thought that social cohesion among the slaves was not totally destroyed. For in one of his studies of Negro life he makes the assertion that the Negro church was "the only social institution among the Negroes which started in the African forest and survived slavery" and that "under the leadership of the priest and medicine man" the church preserved the remnants of African tribal life.[11] From the available evidence, including what we know of the manner in which the slaves were Christianized and the character of their churches, it is impossible to establish any continuity between African religious practices and the Negro church in the United States. It is more likely that what occurred in America was similar to what Mercier has pointed out in

regard to the Fon of Dahomey.[12] His studies showed that with
the breaking up or destruction of the clan and kinship organization, the religious myths and cults lost their significance. In America the destruction of the clan and kinship
organization was more devastating and the Negroes were
plunged into an alien civilization in which whatever
remained of their religious myths and cults had no meaning
whatever.

The Christian Religion Provides a New Basis of Social Cohesion

It is our position that it was not what remained of African
culture or African religious experience but the Christian
religion that provided the new basis of social cohesion. It
follows then that in order to understand the religion of the
slaves, one must study the influence of Christianity in creating solidarity among a people who lacked social cohesion and
a structured social life.

From the beginning of the importation of slaves into the
colonies, Negroes received Christian baptism. The initial
opposition to the christening of Negroes gradually disappeared when laws made it clear that slaves did not become
free through the acceptance of the Christian faith and baptism.[13] Although slaves were regularly baptized and taken
into the Anglican church during the seventeenth century, it
was not until the opening of the eighteenth century that a
systematic attempt was made on the part of the Church of
England to Christianize Negroes in America. This missionary
effort was carried out by the Society for the Propagation of
the Gospel in Foreign Parts which was chartered in England
in 1701.[14] When the Indians in South Carolina proved to be
so hostile to the first missionary sent out by the Society, he
turned his attention to Negro and Indian slaves.

Unfortunately, we do not possess very detailed records on
the religious behavior of the Negroes who became converts to
Christianity through the missionary efforts of the Society,[15]
nor did the missionaries who worked under the auspices of
the Moravians, Quakers, Presbyterians, and Catholics leave
illuminating accounts of the response of the Negro slaves to

their efforts. We do not know, for example, to what extent the converted slaves resumed their old "heathen" ways or combined the new religious practices and beliefs with the old. In this connection it should be noted that the missionaries recognized the difficulty of converting the adult Africans and concentrated their efforts on the children.[16] However, there is no evidence that there was the type of syncretism or fusion of Christian beliefs and practices with African religious ideas and rituals such as one finds in the Candomblé in Brazil.[17] Despite the reported success in the conversion of Negroes, a study of the situation has revealed that only a small proportion of the slaves in the American colonies could be included among even nominal Christians.[18] In fact, the activities of the Anglican missionaries were directed to individuals whose isolation in the great body of slaves was increased.

As Woodson, the Negro historian, has so aptly called it, "The Dawn of the New Day" in the religious development of Negroes occurred when the Methodists and Baptists began proselytizing the blacks.[19] The proselytizing activities on the part of the Methodists and Baptists, as well as the less extensive missionary work of the Presbyterians, were a phase of the Great Awakening which began in New England and spread to the West and South.[20] When the Methodists and Baptists began their revivals in the South, large numbers of Negroes were immediately attracted to this type of religious worship. However, it was not until after the American Revolution that large masses of the Negro population became converts and joined the Methodist and Baptist churches. During the closing years of the eighteenth century the religious revivals in Kentucky and Tennessee tended to reenforce the forms of conversion which characterized the Methodist revivals and were used in some places by the Baptists and Presbyterians.[21]

Why did the Negro slaves respond so enthusiastically to the proselytizing efforts of the Methodists and Baptists? From what has been pointed out concerning the manner in which the slaves were stripped of their cultural heritage, we may dismiss such speculations as the one that it was due to their African background.[22] We are on sounder ground when we note first that the Baptist and Methodist preachers, who lacked the education of the ministers of the Anglican church, appealed to the poor and the ignorant and the outcast. In the crowds that attended the revivals and camp meetings there were numbers of Negroes who found in the fiery message of salvation a hope and a prospect of escape from their earthly woes. Moreover, the emphasis which the preachers placed upon feeling as a sign of conversion found a ready response in the slaves who were repressed in so many ways. Then there were other factors in the situation that caused the slaves to respond to the forms of religious expression provided by the Baptists and Methodists. As we have indicated, the slaves, who had been torn from their homeland and kinsmen and friends and whose cultural heritage was lost, were isolated and broken men, so to speak. In the emotionalism of the camp meetings and revivals some social solidarity, even if temporary, was achieved, and they were drawn into a union with their fellow men. Later, common religious beliefs and practices and traditions tended to provide a new basis of social cohesion in an alien environment. We shall have more to say about this as we analyze further the development of religion among the slaves.

Not only did religion draw the Negroes into a union with their fellow men, it tended to break down barriers that isolated them morally from their white masters. Where the plantation tended to become a social as well as an industrial institution, the Negro slaves participated in the religious life of their masters. It was part of the discipline on many plantations to provide for the religious instruction of slaves. The house servants often attended the family prayers. As a rule, the galleries in the white churches were reserved for the Negro slaves.[23] The master, and more especially mistress, gave religious instruction to the slaves, and white ministers often preached to Negro congregations and supervised their activities. Thus, despite the vast gulf in the status that separated master and slave, participation in the same religious services drew the Negroes out of their moral isolation in the white man's world.

Christianity: A New Orientation Toward Existence

The uprooting of Negroes and the transportation of them to an alien land undoubtedly had a shattering effect upon their lives. In destroying their traditional culture and in breaking up their social organization, slavery deprived them of their accustomed orientation toward the world. Contrary to early misconceptions and still popularly held beliefs concerning the primitiveness of African religions, the peoples from which the slaves were drawn possessed developed systems of religious beliefs concerning their place in nature and in society.[24] In the crisis which they experienced the enslaved Negroes appealed to their ancestors and their gods. But their ancestors and their gods were unable to help them. Some slaves committed suicide during the "middle passage" while others sought the same means of escape from bondage in the new environment.[25] The vast majority of the slaves submitted to their fate and in their confusion and bewilderment sought a meaning for their existence in the new white man's world.

The new orientation to the world was provided by Christianity as communicated to the slaves by their white masters. Naturally, those elements among the slaves who worked and lived in close association with the whites were more influenced by Christian teachings and practices than the slaves who had few contacts with the whites. Those slaves who were largely isolated from the whites engaged in religious practices that undoubtedly included some African survivals. However, the whites were always on guard against African religious practices which could provide an opportunity for slave revolts, and they outlawed such practices. Moreover, there were efforts on the part of the whites to bring the slaves increasingly under the influence of the Christian religion. This was accomplished in part by acquainting the slaves with the Bible.

There were some misgivings and in some instances strong opposition to acquainting the Negro with the Bible. This fear of teaching the slaves the Bible was tied up with the laws against teaching slaves to read and write. But it was also feared that the slave would find in the Bible the implications of human equality which would incite the Negro to make efforts to free himself. Opposition to teaching the Negro the Bible declined as masters became convinced that sufficient justification for slavery could be found in the New Testament. In fact, some masters became convinced that some of the best slaves—that is, those amenable to control by their white masters—were those who read the Bible.[26]

Of course, the illiterate slaves could not gain a first-hand knowledge of the Bible. But for an illiterate people it possessed great influence as a source of supernatural knowledge because it was a sacred book. Perhaps it is safe to say that among no other people has the Bible provided a better illustration of Frazer's statement in the preface of the second edition of his *Passages of the Bible* than among the Negroes of the United States. Especially is this true when he speaks of "the pathetic associations with which the faith and piety of many generations have invested the familiar words" and that it strengthens man in "the blind conviction, or the trembling hope that somewhere, beyond these earthly shadows, there is a world of light eternal, where obstinate questionings of the mind will be answered and the heart find rest." [27]

By this statement we do not intend to give the impression that the Negroes completely assimilated the moral idealism of Christianity or even understood the language of the Bible. Selected parts of the Bible, such as the Lord's Prayer and the Ten Commandments, were used by the masters for the religious instruction of the slaves. In addition, stories from the Bible were told in simple language to the slaves. The slaves became familiar with the well-known biblical characters and their role in the drama of salvation as it was presented to the Negro. Through the medium of the Negro preacher the stories in the Bible were dramatized for the Negro and many characters and incidents were interpreted in terms of the Negro's experiences.

The Bible was the means by which the Negroes acquired a new theology. As we have noted, the Negroes who were brought to the New World undoubtedly carried memories of their gods. These memories were lost or forgotten and there was a determined effort on the part of the whites to prevent any resurgence of African religion. It was from the Bible that the slaves learned of the god of the white man and of his ways with the world and with men. The slaves were taught that the God with whom they became acquainted in the Bible was the ruler of the universe and superior to all other gods. They were taught that the God of the Bible punished and rewarded black men as well as white men. Black men were expected to accept their lot in this world and if they were obedient and honest and truthful they would be rewarded in the world after death. In a book of sermons and dialogues prepared by a minister of the Protestant Episcopal Church in Maryland in 1743 for use by masters and mistresses in their families, the slave in the dialogue says: "God will reward me; and indeed I have good reason to be content and thankful; and I sometimes think more so than if I was free and ever so rich and great; for then I might be tempted to love and serve myself more than God. . . . But now I can't help knowing my duty. I am to serve God in that state in which he has placed me. I am to do what my master orders me." [28]

In providing a theology, and thereby a new orientation toward the world and man, the Bible provided the Negro with the rich imagery which has characterized the sermons of Negro preachers and the sacred folk songs of the Negro.

The Negro Adapts Christianity to His Experience in the New World

The Negro slave found in Christianity a theology and a new orientation toward the world at large and in doing so he adapted the Christian religion to his psychological and social needs. One of the best sources of information on the manner in which the Negro adapted Christianity to his peculiar psychological and social needs is to be found in that great body of sacred folk music known as the "Negro Spirituals." In recent years there have been some efforts on the part of Negro intellectuals, encouraged sometimes by white radicals, to invest most of the Spirituals with a revolutionary meaning or to claim that they represented disguised plans for escape from slavery.[29] It is our position that the sacred folk songs or Spirituals were essentially religious in sentiment and, as we shall see, otherworldly in outlook. We are aware that since the Spirituals are folk songs they underwent changes which make it impossible to know what they were originally. Moreover, we are not unaware of the interpretations which often reflect the biases of whites.

We recognize too that some of the folk songs were undoubtedly composed for special occasions and, therefore, cannot be understood completely outside the framework of a particular time and place. Nevertheless, the sacred folk songs express the awe and wonder of the Negro in regard to life and death and his emotional reactions to the complexity of his existence and his desire to escape from the uncertainties and frustrations of this world.

On the Sea Islands off the coast of South Carolina and Georgia where the slaves were most isolated from whites, some of the Spirituals reveal some continuity with their African background. This continuity is to be found especially in what has been called the Afro-American shout songs.[30] These shout songs are so named because they were sung and are still sung while the Negro worshippers are engaged in what might be called a holy dance. This may be regarded as an example of the most primitive and elemental expression of religion among American Negroes. Moreover, it provides an excellent illustration of Marett's contention that primitive man "does not preach his religion, but dances it instead."[31] Although the shout songs most likely reveal a connection with the African background, they were addressed to the "Good Lord," or the white man's god. The influence of Christian ideology is revealed in other ways. These songs contain the idea of heaven and a judgment day when Gabriel will blow his trumpet.

In fact, in most of the Spirituals which have been gathered from all areas in the South, Christian ideology or theology is evident in practically all of them. The Christian theology is revealed in the Negro's conception of the world. His conception of the world is a world ruled by the Providence of an almighty God.[32] According to the words of one Spiritual:

> My God is a rock in a weary land,
> My God is a rock in a weary land,
> Shelter in time of storm.

From the standpoint of his earthly condition, the Negro was constantly concerned with death. In a recent lecture dealing with the Spirituals, a distinguished Negro minister has pointed out that for the slave death was an ever-present and compelling fact "because of the cheapness with which his life was regarded. The slave was a tool, a thing, a utility, a commodity, but he was not a person. He was faced constantly with the imminent threat of death, of which the terrible overseer was the symbol; and the awareness that he (the slave) was only chattel property, the dramatization."[33]

One only needs to recall the words of many of the Spirituals to realize how important death was to the slaves and later to the emancipated Negro. Their concern with death is shown in the following words of a Spiritual [34] in which the worshippers sing:

> Come down, come down, my Lord,
> An' take me up to wear de crown.

And let us note that:

> My Lord's writin' all de time
> He sees all you do, hears all you say.

Death was not only always at hand, but it was also a terrible experience because God holds one accountable for the way in which one has behaved in this world.

> Death is gwinter lay his cold icy hands on me, Lord.
> Death is gwinter lay his cold icy hands on me,
> One mornin' I was walkin' along
> I heard a voice and saw no man;
> Said go in peace and sin no more,
> Yo' sins fo'given an' yo' soul set free.
> One of dese mornin's it won't be long,
> Yo'll look fo' me an' I'll be gone.[35]

The concern with death is connected with the predominantly other-worldly outlook in the Negro's religion. In many of the Spirituals death appears as a means of escape from the woes and weariness of this world. The words of an often sung Spiritual say that:

> By and by, I'm goin' to lay down this heavy load.
> By and by, by and by, I'm goin' to lay down this heavy load.[36]

Then when those who are "saved" reach heaven, the words of another Spiritual read:

> I've got a robe, you've got a robe,
> All God's children got a robe,
> When I get to heaven goin' to put on my robe
> Goin' to shout all over God's heaven.[37]

For a people who had been separated from kinsmen and friends, it was inevitable that the ties of kinship formed in the New World should be the most valued form of human association. This was especially true in respect to the relationship between the mother and her children since, generally, no recognition was accorded the relationship between spouses and the father and his children. The words of a Spiritual tell of relatives in heaven:

> I've got a mother in de heaven,
>   Outshines de sun,
> I've got a father in de heaven,
>   Outshines de sun,
> I've got a sister in de heaven,
>   Outshines de sun,
> When we get to heaven, we will
>   Outshine de sun,
>   Way beyond de moon.[38]

As we have shown, the Negro slaves were lonely men. It was often in their loneliness that religion was a solace in that they could escape from their loneliness by communicating with God. The slaves would speak of walking and talking with God. They often became converted and found salvation when God spoke to them and told them that they were free of sin. Nevertheless, the slave, without secure family ties, was aware of his loneliness in this world. In response to this feeling of loneliness the slave might sing:

> Sometimes I feel like a motherless child,
> Sometimes I feel like a motherless child,
> A long ways from home.[39]

Or, perhaps, the religious implications of his loneliness were expressed in the words of another Spiritual.

> An' I couldn't hear nobody pray, O Lord,
> O, way down yonder by myself and I couldn't hear nobody pray,
> Wid my burden, I couldn't hear nobody pray.[40]

More often, however, the religion of the Negro was expressed in the Spirituals showing faith and fellowship with his fellow slaves.

> I'm gwine to jine de great 'sociation,
> I'm gwine to jine de great 'sociation.
> Den my little soul's gwine to shine.

The great 'sociation was, at least as its earthly manifestations were concerned, the "invisible institution" of the Negro church.

The "Invisible Institution" Comes into Existence

It is no exaggeration to say that the "invisible institution" of the Negro church took root among the enslaved blacks. The key to an understanding of the "invisible institution" may be found in the typical remark of an ex-slave who wrote:

> Our preachers were usually plantation folks just like the rest of us. Some man who had a little education and had been taught something about the Bible would be our preacher. The colored folks had their code of religion, not nearly so complicated as the white man's religion, but more closely observed. . . . When we had our meetings of this kind, we held them in our own way and were not interfered with by the white folks.[41]

The observation of a Swedish visitor to the New World sheds more light upon the manner in which the "invisible institution" of the Negro Church was accomplished. Concerning a visit near Charleston in 1851, she wrote:

> in the village itself everything was still and quiet. A few Negro men and women were standing about, and they looked kind and well to do. I heard

in one house a sound as of prayer and zealous exhortation. I entered, and saw the assemblage of Negroes, principally women, who were much edified and affected in listening to a Negro who was preaching to them with great fervor and great gesticulation, thumping on the table with his clenched fists. The sermon and substance of his sermon was this: "Let us do as Christ has commanded us; let us love one another. Then he will come to us on our sickbeds, on our deathbeds, and he will make us free, and we shall come to him and sit with him in glory." [42]

Since all forms of organized social effort were forbidden among the slaves and in the absence of an established priesthood, the Negro preacher played the important role in the "invisible institution" of the church among the slaves. The Negro preacher was "called" to his office and through his personal qualities achieved a position of dominance. The "call" was supposed to have come through some religious experience which indicated that God had chosen him as a spiritual leader. According to Frederick Douglass, the abolitionist orator who escaped from slavery, the preacher was one of the slave notabilities.[43] The preacher to whom Douglass refers seems to have achieved his authority because of personal qualities. This authority was given greater weight when the slave who had been called to preach was licensed by the Methodist or Baptist Church.

One qualification which the Negro preacher among the slaves needed to possess was some knowledge of the Bible. However imperfect or distorted his knowledge of the Bible might be, the fact that he was acquainted with the source of sacred knowledge, which was in a sense the exclusive possession of his white masters, gave him prestige in matters concerning the supernatural and religious among his fellow slaves. His knowledge of the sacred scriptures had to be combined with an ability to speak and communicate his special knowledge to the slaves. As one white minister pointed out, the religious instruction of the slaves required preaching rather than instruction in the Christian faith. Preaching meant dramatizing the stories of the Bible and the way of God to man. These slave preachers were noted for the imagery of their sermons. One slave preacher, John Jasper, achieved distinction, according to his biographer, because of his lofty dignity which was combined with his fiery and thrilling oratory despite his "tempestuous and ungrammatical eloquence." [44]

Another qualification which the slave preacher must possess was the ability to sing. From the beginning of religious expression among the slaves which was characterized by the "shout songs," preaching on the part of the leader was important. This preaching consisted of singing sacred songs which have come to be known as the Spirituals. The singing of these preachers and for that matter preachers among the Negro masses later has been a sort of "moaning." [45] Usually, the singing of the Spirituals has accompanied the "shouting" or holy dancing which has characterized this ecstatic form of religious worship among Negroes.

The Negro preacher among the slaves was more than a leader in these ephemeral gatherings whose members were held together by the emotional contagion which Marett has called the "mobish" character of primitive religions. [46] Because of the local autonomy in Baptist churches in contrast to the centralized hierarchy of the Methodist church, the Negro preacher was free to exercise his gifts and to direct his followers. This also accounts in part at least for the larger number of slaves who were attracted to the Baptists. The leadership of the preacher was recognized by his "congregation" and as far as the white masters were willing to concede to him this role among the slaves. Although the masters were unwilling to tolerate any form of organized activities among the slaves, different members of the "congregations" played various roles according to their talents as singers or according to their ability to influence other slaves to get converted or attend religious services.

The recognition which the whites accorded to the Negro "congregations" was accorded them as segments of the white organizations. White control of these segments was never completely relaxed. Therefore, there was always some tension because the slaves preferred their own preachers and wanted to conduct their religious services according to their own mode of worshipping. This tension was always sharpened by the fact that there were free Negroes in the churches which were established in connection with the white church organizations. The tension was never resolved and the Negro church never emerged as an independent institution except under the Negroes who were free before the Civil War.

2

THE INSTITUTIONAL CHURCH OF THE FREE NEGROES

Negroes Who Were Free Before the Civil War

THE twenty Negroes who were sold to the Virginia settlers by a Dutch man-of-war in 1619 were not slaves, since there was no precedent in English law for slavery. These Negroes and those imported later were "absorbed in a growing system (servitude based upon English apprenticeship and vagrancy laws) which spread to all the colonies and for nearly a century furnished the chief supply of colonial labor."[1] Little is known of what became of the first twenty Negroes who were introduced into the Virginia colony. However, there is a record of the baptism of a child of one couple among them. This is significant because at the time, according to the law of England by which the colony was governed, "a slave who had been christened or baptized became 'infranchised.' "[2] It appears that the original twenty Negroes were freed after seven years of indentured labor and that at least one among them, an Anthony Johnson, acquired considerable land after becoming free. As the enslavement of Negroes developed in practice and was confirmed by law, during the seventeenth century, Maryland as well as Virginia passed laws to the effect that Christian baptism did not confer freedom upon the slaves.

Nevertheless, the free Negro population in the colonies and later in the United States continued to increase until the outbreak of the Civil War. The increase in the free Negro population came from five sources: (1) children born of free colored persons; (2) mulatto children born of colored mothers; (3) mulatto children born of white servants or free women; (4) children of free Negro and Indian parentage; and (5) slaves who were set free.[3] It is difficult to estimate the proportion of the increase in the number of free Negroes attributable to each source. The growth in numbers resulting from natural increase continued until the Civil War. On the other hand, the accessions to the free Negro population through the unions of free and servant white women and white men were kept at a minimum because of the drastic laws against such unions.[4] Although there was constant intermixture of Negroes and Indians in areas reserved for Indians as well as outside these areas, there is no way of knowing to what extent this intermixture contributed to the growth of the free Negro population.

It appears that the manumission or the freeing of slaves was the main source through which the free Negro population increased. This was accomplished both by public and private action. Occasionally, public manumission came as a reward for some meritorious public service such as revealing a Negro conspiracy. A Pierre Chastang of Mobile, Alabama, was bought and freed by popular subscription in recognition of his services in the War of 1812 and in the yellow fever epidemic in 1819.[5] It is probable that some of the fervor in emancipating the slaves was due to the philosophy of the Revolution. This was the case in the North, at least, where slavery had no real economic base and was dying out. In the Southern States, Maryland and Virginia, there were legal restrictions upon private emancipation which was the means by which masters sometimes relieved themselves of slaves who could no longer be worked for profit.

The Negroes who were free before the Civil War were concentrated in the areas where the plantation system of agriculture either had not taken root or had died out. They were to be found chiefly in the tidewater region of Virginia and Maryland and the Piedmont region of North Carolina. Moreover, there were settlements of free Negroes in the North and in the isolated communities of Negroes mixed with Indians. But the majority of free Negroes were concentrated in

the cities both in the North and in the South. It was in the
urban areas of the South that the free Negroes were able to
achieve a secure position in the economic organization. On
the other hand, in the cities of the North, the free Negroes
were confronted with the competition of European immigrants and had a difficult time in surviving. In the North
the free Negroes could acquire some education openly while
in the South they had to secure education surreptitiously and
through their own efforts. Since many free Negroes acquired
their freedom as the result of being children of free colored
women and white men or slave women and white men who
emancipated their colored offspring, nearly two-fifths of the
free Negroes were mulattoes or of mixed ancestry. In the cities
of the South, especially in Charleston, South Carolina, and in
New Orleans, the communities of free mulattoes became almost an intermediate caste between the whites and the slaves.
They acquired considerable wealth, including slaves; they
maintained conventional standards of sex and family life;
they were cultivated people who often sent their children to
Europe for education and in order to escape racial prejudice.

Among the free Negroes in both the North and the South,
there developed an organized community life. Most of their
efforts were concerned with mutual aid societies and
cooperation for economic welfare. These organizations,
including efforts to acquire an education, were generally tied
up with their churches which comprised a large part of their
wealth.[6] Their church organizations had come into existence
as the result of the proselytizing activities on the part of
whites but had become important as the result of the efforts
of the free Negroes themselves.

Relation of Free Negroes and Whites in the Churches

The relations of free Negroes and whites in the churches
were determined largely by the slave status of the majority of
the Negro population. Although the Anglican Church, as we
have seen, carried on missionary activities among the slaves,
they were not interested in changing the status of Negro
slaves. It was the Quakers who in accepting both Negro slaves

and free men on a basis of equality became the enemies of the system of slavery. As early as the seventeenth century the Quakers advocated the religious training of the slaves as a preparation for freedom. Many of the Quakers freed their slaves and helped to remove legal restrictions against the private manumission of slaves. The relation of the free Negroes to the whites in the churches did not become a real issue until the Negroes were evangelized by the Methodists and Baptists.

Among the early Baptist and Methodist missionaries, there were many who preached the liberation of the slave as a part of their creed. The Methodists required their traveling missionaries to set slaves free on the ground that slavery was contrary to the laws of God, man, and nature.[7] In 1784 the Methodist conference took steps towards the abolition of slavery, declaring that slavery was opposed to the laws of God and contrary to the principles of the American Revolution. However, the Baptists were winning more Negroes in their local meetings by their open attack on slavery. Gradually, both the Methodists and the Baptists receded from their position in face of the general opposition to their stand on the question of slavery.

The relation of the free Negroes to the white Christian churches may be seen first in the activities of the early Negro preachers and their relations with white congregations. This was natural since, as we have seen, the Negro preacher, slave as well as free, occupied a dominant position in the religious activities of Negroes. The traditional African priesthood had disappeared and a church organization only grew up gradually among the Negroes. The oldest or next to the oldest Negro Baptist church to be established in the United States was due to the efforts of George Liele, a slave born in Virginia about 1750 and taken by his master to Georgia before the Revolutionary War.[8] As the result of accompanying his master, who was a deacon, to church he was converted and baptized. Because of his "unusual ministerial gifts," he was permitted to preach on the plantations and later he was liberated by his master to carry on his work as a minister. His master was killed in the Revolutionary War and when the heirs raised some question about his free status, Liele followed the British when they evacuated Savannah. Before leaving Savannah, he baptized Andrew Bryan and some other Negroes who became the founders of the African Baptist Church in Savannah.

Andrew Bryan was born a slave in South Carolina and was brought by his master to Savannah. He began with public exhortations and prayer meetings and was soon preaching to congregations of white and black people in Savannah. Bryan was permitted by his master and other whites to erect a church. But considerable opposition developed because it was feared that despite the "salutary" effect of his preaching, the religious gatherings would lead to a slave uprising. Bryan and his brother suffered considerable persecution including whippings and torture. His master came to his defense, and he was permitted to conduct his services in a barn. Through the assistance of influential friends he was able to collect funds in order to purchase a lot upon which he built a church. When his master died, the heirs of the estate gave him an opportunity to purchase his freedom. However, the church remained under the control of the heirs of his master's estate and the worship of the communicants continued to be supervised by whites. As the membership increased a number of congregations split and new churches were founded. When Bryan died in 1812, he was the acknowledged and respected leader of the religious life of Negroes in Georgia.

The pioneering work of Negro Baptist preachers was more successful in those areas of the South where the interests of the ruling whites were not so deeply rooted in the plantation system. This was especially true in the cities of Virginia where a number of Baptist churches were established in the last decade of the eighteenth century and during the early years of the nineteenth century. Moreover, there were outstanding Negro preachers who had embraced the Methodist faith and were pioneers in establishing congregations among their fellow slaves and freedmen. One famous Negro preacher, known as Black Harry and described as "small, very black, keen-eyed, possessing great volubility of tongue," accompanied Asbury and was declared by Dr. Benjamin Rush to be the greatest orator in America.[9] Black Harry and other Negro Methodist preachers, as many Negro Baptist preachers had done, preached to white as well as Negro congregations. But there was always some question concerning the propriety of Negroes preaching to whites. There was even opposition to whites and Negroes worshipping together. What happened in the case of a Negro preacher in Northampton, Virginia, toward the end of the eighteenth century may be taken as typical. The white Baptist association stated that "whereas the black brethren in the church seemed anxious for a vote in the conference that it would be best to consider the black people as a wing of the body," [10] and that Josiah Bishop, a famous Negro preacher who had been pastor of the mixed congregation, be assigned pastor of the black congregation. The Negro communicants did not press their desire to vote and continued in their subordinate position. Josiah Bishop went to Baltimore and later to New York to become pastor of the Abyssinian Baptist Church.

Conflict over the Question of Status

It is apparent then that in the early development of the Negro church on an institutional basis there was the question of the status of the Negro preachers and Negro communicants in relation to the white church organizations. In the South where slavery was the normal condition of the Negro or as the Supreme Court of Mississippi stated that the laws of the State "presume a Negro *prima facie* to be a slave," it was to be expected that the question of the status of the Negro in the churches should be insistent. In fact, the schism which was created in the various national church organizations over the question of slavery involved the status of the Negro in the Christian churches. After many attempts to reconcile the viewpoint of the southern sections of these church organizations which sought justification of slavery in the Scriptures with that of northern elements who refused to justify slavery on Christian grounds, the Methodists, Baptists, and Presbyterians split and set up separate organizations. In the South the Negroes continued to join the Methodist and Baptist churches in large numbers and to worship in the segregated sections of the churches of their masters. In many places, the situation in Charleston, South Carolina, being typical, the Presbyterians and Episcopalians built separate churches for their Negro members. As the Negro membership increased, the Baptists and Methodists too provided their Negro members with separate churches. In these separate church organizations the Negroes tended to conduct their services according to their own mode of religious expression though under white supervision. But there was always an urge to achieve a certain degree of autonomy on the part of Negro congregations.

The question of status was not confined to the South.[11] In the North as in the South a number of Negro preachers had acquired some distinction and had preached to predominantly white congregations. Among these was Lemuel Haynes, the illegitimate child of a Negro and a white woman who was born in Connecticut in 1753. He took the name of a white benefactor who took him in his home when he was abandoned by his mother. Haynes grew to manhood in Massachusetts after having been bound out as a child of five months. It was in the home of the man to whom he was bound out that he first read the Bible and conducted the family prayers. He was licensed to preach in the Congregational Church and serve in a number of churches in New England.[12]

The most famous of the Negro preachers in the North was, in a sense, Richard Allen because of the role which he played in the organization of an independent Negro church organization.[13] Allen was born a slave in Philadelphia but was sold to a planter who took him to Delaware. He early came under the influence of Methodist preachers and was converted in 1777. He was allowed to conduct prayers and preach in the house of his master who became converted. In the same year, he and his brother were permitted to purchase their freedom from their master, who had become convinced that slavery was wrong, for $2000 in depreciated Continental currency.[14]

After becoming free, Allen engaged in odd jobs but remained intensely religious and became a preacher in 1780. In recognition of his talents as a preacher he was allowed to travel with white ministers and given assignments by Bishop Asbury When he went to Philadelphia in 1786 he was invited to preach in the St. George Methodist Episcopal Church. When Allen observed in Philadelphia the need of the Negroes for religious leadership and an organization, he proposed that a separate church be established for Negroes. His proposal was opposed both by whites and Negroes. However, when the number of Negroes attending St. George Methodist Episcopal Church increased, Negroes were removed from the seats around the wall and ordered to sit in the gallery. Mistaking the section of the gallery which they were to occupy, Allen, Absalom Jones, and another member were almost dragged from their knees as they prayed.[15] They left the church and together with other Negro members founded the Free African Society.

The Free Negroes Establish Their Own Churches

After Richard Allen and Absalom Jones organized the Free African Society, they differed as to whether Negroes should model their church organization after the Methodist or after the Protestant Episcopal Church. Allen was of the opinion that the Methodist form of worship was more suited to the religious needs and form of worship to which the Negroes had become accustomed. As a consequence of this difference between Jones and Allen, Jones organized the African Protestant Episcopal Church of St. Thomas but the majority of the Negroes who had seceded from the white church followed Allen. Allen organized the Bethel Church for which an old building was purchased and dedicated in 1794. Bishop Asbury ordained Allen a deacon and later he became an elder. The movement begun by Allen under the name of African societies spread to other cities where so-called African Methodist Episcopal Churches were set up. There was some cooperation among the leaders of the separate church organizations in the various cities. As a result, the representatives of these churches met in Philadelphia in 1816 and established the African Methodist Episcopal Church. At this meeting Allen was elected bishop and a book of discipline was adopted which embodied the same articles of religion and rules as the Wesleyans.[16]

The secession of Negroes from the white Methodist church in Philadelphia was followed by secessions in New York City. Peter Williams, Sr., whose son became the first Negro to be ordained as a priest in the Protestant Episcopal Church, was himself a sexton for a number of years in the John Street Methodist Church. He was distinguished for his piety and faithfulness among the white communicants. However, being influenced by the general movement among Negroes to establish their own churches, he joined with other Negroes in organizing the Zion Church out of which developed the African Methodist Episcopal Zion Church. During this period independent Baptist churches were being established by Negroes in the Southern States, Maryland, Virginia, Georgia, and Kentucky, and in northern cities, Boston, New York City, and Philadelphia. It was only much later that these Negro Baptist churches were brought together in a national convention. On a much smaller scale Negroes organized Protestant Episcopal, Presbyterian, and Congregational churches. As the result of Emancipation still another Negro Methodist organization came into existence. When the split occurred in the Methodist Church in 1844 over the question of slavery, the Negroes continued, as we have seen, to join and worship in the churches of their masters while in the North there were Negro congregations which continued to be connected with the Methodist Episcopal Church. After the Civil War, the small Negro membership which remained in the Methodist Episcopal Church South was permitted to organize a separate body. Thus, there came into existence the Colored Methodist Episcopal Church in Jackson, Tennessee, in 1870. In these various Methodist and Baptist church organizations, nearly a half of the Negroes have remained, on the whole, to the present day.

3

THE NEGRO CHURCH: A NATION WITHIN A NATION

The "Invisible Institution" Merges with the Institutional Church

THE Civil War and Emancipation destroyed whatever stability and order that had developed among Negroes under the slave régime. An educated mulatto minister of the African Methodist Episcopal Church who went from the North to the South following Emancipation wrote:

> The whole section (in the neighborhood of Charleston, South Carolina) with its hundreds of thousands of men, women and children just broken forth from slavery, was, so far as these were concerned, dying under an almost physical and moral interdict. There was no one to baptize their children, to perform marriage, or to bury the dead. A ministry had to be created at once—created out of the material at hand.[1]

The "material at hand" was, of course, those Negroes among the slaves who had been "called to preach." In answer to the criticism that neither men nor money were available for creating a ministry, the minister just quoted wrote that "God could call the men; and that the A.M.E. Church had the authority to commission them when thus called." This represented the fusion of the "invisible institution" of the Negro church which had taken root among the slaves and the institutional church which had grown up among the Negroes who were free before the Civil War.

The most obvious result of the merging of the "invisible institution" of the church which had grown up among the slaves with the institutional church of the Negroes who were free before the Civil War was the rapid growth in the size of the Negro church organization. But there was a much more important result of this merger which is of primary concern to our study. The merger resulted in the structuring or organization of Negro life to an extent that had not existed. This becomes clear when we recall that organized social life among the transplanted Negroes had been destroyed by slavery. The traditional African clan and family had been destroyed and in the environment of the New World the development of a structured family life was always nullified by the exigencies of the plantation system. Any efforts toward organization in their religious life was prevented because of the fear of the whites of slave insurrections. Even any spontaneous efforts toward mutual aid on an organized basis was prevented for the same reasons. There was, to be sure, some social differentiation among the slaves based upon the different roles which they played in the plantation economy. But this did not result in the structuring of the social life among the slaves themselves. Among the slaves themselves one may note the germs of stratification based upon their different roles in the plantation, but no system of stratification ever came into existence that became the basis of an organized social existence.

This was all changed when the Negro became free, and it is our purpose here to show how an organized religious life became the chief means by which a structured or organized social life came into existence among the Negro masses. The process by which the "invisible institution" of the slaves merged with the institutional churches built by the free Negroes had to overcome many difficulties. These difficulties arose chiefly from the fact that there were among the free Negroes many mulattoes and that they, as well as the unmixed Negroes, represented a higher degree of assimilation of white or European culture. This was often reflected in the difference in the character of the religious services of those with a background of freedom and those who were just released from slavery. In fact, in the social stratification of the Negro population after Emancipation, a free and mulatto ancestry became the basis of important social distinctions.[2] It should be pointed out, however, that these cultural and social distinctions were reflected in the denominational affiliation of Negroes. The Negro masses were concentrated in the Methodist and Baptist churches which provided for a more emotional and ecstatic form of worship than the Protestant Episcopal, Presbyterian, and Congregational churches. But even in the Methodist and Baptist denominations there were separate church organizations based upon distinctions of color and what were considered standards of civilized behavior. In the Methodist and Baptist churches in which the vast majority of Negroes were communicants, it was impractical to organize separate churches which would be congenial to the way of life of the small Negro élite. Nevertheless, some of the educated leaders were not in sympathy with the more primitive religious behavior of the masses. The attitude of educated leaders of even Methodist and Baptist churches was expressed by a Bishop in the African Methodist Episcopal Church even before Emancipation. He opposed the singing of the Spirituals, which he described as "corn field ditties" and songs of "fist and heel worshippers" and said that the ministry of the A.M.E. Church must drive out such "heathenish mode of worship" or "drive out all intelligence and refinement."[3]

Despite the difficulties, the integration of the "invisible institution" which had emerged among the slaves into the Negro church organization established by the free Negroes was achieved. This provided an organization and structuring of Negro life which has persisted until the present time. We shall begin by considering the relation of the organization of the religious life of the Negro to building up of social control.

The Church as an Agency of Social Control

In dealing with the Negro church as an agency of control we shall focus attention upon the relation of the church to the Negro family and sex life during the years following Emancipation. In order to understand the important role of the Negro church, it is necessary to have a clear conception of the situation which confronted organized religion. Under slavery the Negro family was essentially an amorphous group gathered around the mother or some female on the plantation. The father was a visitor to the household without any legal or recognized status in family relations. He might disappear as the result of the sale of slaves or because of a whimsical change of his own feelings or affection. Among certain favored elements on the plantation, house slaves and skilled artisans, the family might achieve greater stability and the father and husband might develop a more permanent interest in his family. Whatever might be the circumstances of the Negro family under the slave régime, family and sex relations were constantly under the supervision of the whites.

The removal of the authority of masters as the result of the Civil War and Emancipation caused promiscuous sex relations to become widespread and permitted the constant changing of spouses. The daughter of a planter family who has idealized the slave régime nevertheless tells a story which illustrates the disorder. "Mammy Maria," she wrote, "came out in the new country as 'Miss Dabney,' and attracted, as she informed her 'white children,' as much admiration as any of the young girls, and had offers of marriage too. But she meant to enjoy her liberty, she said, and should not think of marrying any of them."[4] Some of the confusion in marital relations was due, of course, to the separation of husbands and wives during slavery and the social disorganization that resulted from Emancipation.

The problem of monogamous and stable family life was one of the most vexing problems that confronted northern white missionaries who undertook to improve the morals of the newly liberated blacks. These missionaries undertook to persuade the freedmen to legalize and formalize their marriages. There was resistance on the part of many of the slaves since legal marriage was not in their mores. Sometimes missionaries even attempted to use force in order that the freedmen legalize their sexual unions. There were, of course, many cases in which the marriage ceremony was a confirmation of a union that was based upon conjugal sentiment established over a long period of association. Marriage and an institutional family life could not be imposed by white missionaries. Marriage and the family could acquire an institutional character only as the result of the operation of economic and social forces within the Negro communities.

A large proportion of the Negro families among the freedmen continued after Emancipation to be dependent upon the Negro mother as they had been during slavery. But the new economic conditions which resulted from Emancipation tended to place the Negro man in a position of authority in family relations. The freedmen refused to work in gangs as they had done during slavery, and a man would take his wife and children and rent and operate a farm on his own account.[5] The man or husband in the family was required to sign the rent or work agreements. Sometimes the wives were also required to sign but the husband or father was always held responsible for the behavior of his family. The more stable elements among the freedmen who had been in a position to assimilate the sentiments and ideas of their former masters soon undertook to buy land. This gave the husband and father an interest in his wife and children that no preaching on the part of white missionaries or Negro preachers could give. But it would be a serious mistake to overlook the manner in which the new economic position of the man was consolidated by the moral support of the Negro church.

There was, of course, moral support for a patriarchal family to be found in the Bible and this fact contributed undoubtedly a holy sanction to the new authority of the Negro man in the family. However, there were more important ways in which the Negro church gave support to Negro family life with the father in a position of authority. As we have pointed out, after Emancipation the Negro had to create a new communal life or become integrated into the communities created by the Negroes who were free before the Civil War. Generally, this resulted in the expansion and complete transformation of these communities. The leaders in creating a new community life were men who with their families worked land or began to buy land or worked as skilled artisans. It is important to observe that these pioneers in the creation of a communal life generally built a church as well as homes. Many of these pioneer leaders were preachers who gathered their communicants about them and became the leaders of the Negro communities. This fact tends to reveal the close relationship between the newly structured life of the Negro and his church organizations.

The churches became and have remained until the past twenty years or so, the most important agency of social control among Negroes. The churches undertook as organizations to censure unconventional and immoral sex behavior and to punish by expulsion sex offenders and those who violated the monogamous mores. But it was impossible to change immediately the loose and unregulated sex and family behavior among a people lacking the institutional basis of European sexual mores. Very often the churches had to tolerate or accommodate themselves to sexual irregularities.[6] A bishop in the African Methodist Episcopal Church in recounting the task of "cleaning up" irregular sex behavior among the members of the church where he served said that his church became "the Ecclesiastical Court House, as well as the Church."[7] Let us not forget, however, the control exercised by the Negro was exercised by dominating personalities. Frequently, they were the preachers who had become leaders of Negroes because of their talents and ability to govern men. Very often they were self-made men.[8] In the Baptist Churches in which the majority of the Negroes have always been concentrated there was even greater opportunity for self-assertion and the assumption of leadership on the part of strong men. This naturally resulted in a pattern of autocratic leadership which has spilled over into most aspects of organized social life among Negroes, especially in as much as many forms of organized social life have grown out of the church and have come under the dominant leadership of Negro preachers.

The Church and Economic Cooperation

As DuBois pointed out more than fifty years ago, "a study of economic cooperation among Negroes must begin with the Church group."[9] It was in order to establish their own churches that Negroes began to pool their meager economic resources and buy buildings and the land on which they stood. As an indication of the small beginnings of these churches, we may note that the value of the property of the African Methodist Episcopal Church in 1787 was only $2500. During the next century the value of the property of this organization increased to nine million dollars.[10] The Negroes in the other Methodist denominations, and especially in the numerous Baptist Churches, were contributing on a similar scale a part of their small earnings for the construction of churches. At the same time, out of the churches grew mutual aid societies. The earliest society of this type was the Free African Society, which was organized in Philadelphia in 1787.[11] We have already noted that the Society was organized by Absalom Jones and Richard Allen, the two Negroes who led the secession from the Methodist Church. At the time the Society was organized, Negroes were migrating to Philadelphia in large numbers and the need for some sort of mutual aid was becoming urgent. The Society became a "curious sort of ethical and beneficial brotherhood" under the direction of Jones and Allen who exercised a "parental discipline" over its members. The avowed purpose of this organization was to "support one another in sickness, and for the benefit of their widows and fatherless children."

In the cities throughout the United States numerous beneficial societies were organized to provide assistance in time of sickness or death.[12] Many of these beneficial societies, like the Free African Society, were connected with churches. These societies continued to be established throughout the nineteenth century. For example, in Atlanta in 1898 there were nine beneficial societies which had been founded from soon after the Civil War up to 1897.[13] Six of these beneficial societies were connected with churches. The names of these beneficial societies are not without significance. At the Wheat Street Baptist Church, for example, there were two beneficial societies—the Rising Star and the Sisters of Love, while at the Bethel (Methodist) Church was the Daughters of Bethel. These associations for mutual aid, which were generally known as beneficial societies, were often the germ out of which grew the secular insurance companies.

The role of religion and the Negro church in more elementary forms of economic cooperation among Negroes may be seen more clearly in the rural mutual aid societies that sprang up among freedmen after Emancipation. They were formed among the poor, landless Negroes who were thrown upon their own resources. These societies were organized to meet the crises of life—sickness and death; consequently, they were known as "sickness and burial" societies. The important fact for our study is that these benevolent societies grew out of the Negro church and were inspired by the spirit of Christian charity. They were supported by the pennies which the Negroes could scrape together in order to aid each other in time of sickness but more especially to insure themselves a decent Christian burial. The influence of the simple religious conceptions of the Negro folk and the Bible is revealed in the names of these mutual aid societies which continue to exist in the rural South. They bear such names as "Love and Charity," "Builders of the Walls of Jerusalem," "Sons and Daughters of Esther," "Brothers and Sisters of Charity," and "Brothers and Sisters of Love." [14]

These "sickness and burial" societies should be distinguished from the fraternal organizations which played an important role in early economic cooperation among Negroes. Fraternal organizations like the Negro Masonic Lodge and the Odd Fellows came into existence among the free Negroes in the North as the result of the influence of the white fraternal organizations.[15] On the other hand, Negroes began before the outbreak of the Civil War to organize fraternal organizations which reflected their own interests and outlook on life. One such secret society, the Knights of Liberty, was organized by a preacher, Reverend Moses Dickson, who was born in Cincinnati in 1824.[16] This organization was active in the underground railroad and claimed to have nearly 50,000 members in 1856. Dickson joined the Union Army and after the Civil War he disbanded the Knights of Liberty. In 1871 he organized the first Temple and Tabernacle of the Knights and Daughters of Tabor in Independence, Missouri. The object of this secret society was "to help to spread the Christian religion and education" and its members were advised to "acquire real estate, avoid intemperance, and cultivate true manhood." At the end of the nineteenth century this society claimed to have nearly 200,000 members in eighteen jurisdictions scattered from Maine to California and from the Great Lakes to the Gulf of Mexico.

The organization and development of the Grand United Order of True Reformers provides a better example of the manner in which an organization under the leadership of a preacher fired with religious zeal played an important role in economic cooperation and the accumulation of capital. The founder of the organization was a Reverend Washington Browne who was born a slave in Georgia in 1849.[17] During the Civil War he ran away from a new master and made his way to the North where he received a meager education. After Emancipation he returned to Alabama where he joined a movement of the Good Templars against the whisky ring. But after observing the various benevolent and burial societies among Negroes, he decided that Negroes should have a separate organization adapted to their special needs. In 1876 he succeeded in bringing together in a single organization, known as the Grand Fountain of True Reformers, twenty-seven Fountains with 2000 members. Although he was not successful in creating a mutual benefit society, through his paper, *The Reformer*, he attracted the attention of the Organization of True Reformers in Virginia. He was invited to Richmond and became the Grand Worthy Master of the Virginia organization.

The True Reformers organized a variety of enterprises, including a weekly newspaper, a real estate firm, a bank, a hotel, a building and loan association, and a grocery and general merchandising store. The True Reformers took the lead in incorporating an insurance feature in its program for the benefit of its members, an example of which was followed by the other fraternal organizations among Negroes. The insurance ventures failed because they did not have sound actuarial basis and were not under government supervision.[18] Nevertheless, the Negro gained a certain experience and training which prepared him for his more successful business ventures.

The Church and Education

The educational development of Negroes does not reflect to the same extent as their churches and mutual aid associations the racial experience and peculiar outlook on life of Negroes. Education, that is Western or European education, was something totally foreign to the Negro's way of life. This was because, as Woodson has written, "The first real educators to take up the work of enlightening American Negroes were clergymen interested in the propagation of the gospel among the heathen in the new world."[19] In fact, the purpose of education was primarily to transmit to the Negro the religious ideas and practices of an alien culture. In the North the strictly religious content of education was supplemented by other elements, whereas in the South limitations were even placed upon enabling the Negro to read the Bible. By 1850 there were large numbers of Negroes attending schools in northern cities. Then, too, individual Negroes managed to acquire a higher education and most of these were men who were preparing to become ministers.

This does not mean that Negroes took no initiative in setting up schools and acquiring an education. The free Negroes in the cities contributed to the support of schools for Negro children. Generally, the support which the free Negroes provided was greater in southern cities like Baltimore, Washington, and Charleston, South Carolina, than in New York and Philadelphia. As early as 1790, the Brown Fellowship Society in Charleston maintained schools for the free Negro children. An important fact about the schools which the free Negroes maintained was that many of them were Sunday schools. On the eve of the Civil War, "There were then in Baltimore Sunday schools about 600 Negroes. They had formed themselves into a Bible Association, which had been received into the convention of the Baltimore Bible Society. In 1825 the Negroes there had a day and night school giving courses in Latin and French. Four years later there appeared an 'African Free School,' with an attendance of from 150 to 175 every Sunday."[20] Although the Sunday schools represented before the Civil War one of the most important agencies in the education of Negroes, nevertheless the churches through their ministers urged parents to send their children to whatever shools were available.[21]

After Emancipation the initiative on the part of Negroes in providing education for themselves was given a much freer scope. This was because of the great educational crusade which was carried on by northern white missionaries among the freedmen. As the Union armies penetrated the South, the representatives of northern missionary societies and churches sent funds and teachers in the wake of the advancing armies. The majority of the men and women or "school marms," as they were called, were inspired by a high idealism and faith in the intellectual capacity of Negroes. They laid the foundation for or established most of the Negro colleges in the South. Working with the Freedmen's Bureau which was created by an Act of Congress in 1865 to aid the freedmen in assuming the responsibilities of citizens, they also laid the foundation for a public school system for the newly emancipated Negro. It was Negroes trained in these schools supported by northern churches and philanthropy who became the educated leaders among Negroes.

The schools—elementary, secondary, and those which provided the beginnings of college education—were permeated with a religious and moral outlook. The graduates of these schools went forth as missionaries to raise the moral and religious level of the members of their race. Many of the men were preachers or became preachers. A preacher who was a graduate of a Baptist college founded by white missionaries and who had helped to make the bricks for the buildings of the college, said that when he was graduated, the white president addressed him as follows: "I want you to go into the worst spot in this State and build a school and a church."[22] This minister followed the instructions of his white mentor and established the school that provided the primary school and later the only secondary school for Negroes in the country and four Baptist Churches. This is typical of the manner in which the Negro preacher who was often the best-educated man in the community took the initiative in establishing schools.

An educated and distinguished bishop in the African Methodist Episcopal Church who was the father of the most distinguished American Negro painter wrote in his history of the Church in 1867: "For it is one of the brightest pages in the history of our Church, that while the Army of the Union were forcing their victorious passage through the southern land and striking down treason, the missionaries of our Church in the persons of Brown, Lynch, Cain, Handy, Stanford, Steward, and others, were following in their wake and establishing the Church and the school house. . . ." [23] The work of the Negro preacher in establishing schools was especially important since the southern States provided only a pittance of public funds for the education of Negro children. When the Julius Rosenwald Fund contributed to the building of more than 5000 schools for Negroes in the South in order to stimulate the public authorities to appropriate money for Negro schools, Negro churches played an important role in making possible the schools aided by the Rosenwald Fund. Negroes contributed 17 percent of the total cost of the schools which amounted to over $28,000,000. They raised much of their share in this amount through church suppers and programs under the auspices of their churches. [24]

The impetus among Negroes to build institutions of higher education was due primarily to their need for an educated ministry. But the desire on the part of the masses for an educated ministry was far from universal. The masses of Negroes were still impressed by the ignorant and illiterate minister who often boasted that he had not been corrupted by wicked secular learning. Soon after the "invisible institution" of the slaves was integrated into the institutional church, it was feared that a schism would occur in the African Methodist Episcopal Church as the result of the conflict between the ignorant and intelligent elements in the church. [25] Nevertheless, the African Methodist Episcopal Church succeeded in establishing a number of so-called colleges and universities. [26] The African Methodist Episcopal Zion Church and the Colored Methodist Episcopal Church also established schools. The Baptists had to depend upon local efforts. In South Carolina the Negro Baptists who became dissatisfied with the white control of the college for Negroes finally established their own school. [27]

The schools and colleges maintained by the Negro church denominations have never attained a high level as educational institutions. They have generally nurtured a narrow religious outlook and have restricted the intellectual development of Negroes even more than the schools established for Negroes by the white missionaries. This has been due only partly to lack of financial resources. It hardly needs to be emphasized that there was no intellectual tradition among Negroes to sustain colleges and universities. The attendance of Negro students at private colleges has reflected the social stratification of the Negro community. The children of the upper class in the Negro community have generally attended the schools established by the Congregational Church and the better type of schools supported by the white Methodists and Baptists for Negroes. Nevertheless, the Negro church has affected the entire intellectual development and outlook of Negroes. This has been due both to the influence of the Negro church which has permeated every phase of social life and to the influence of the Negro preacher whose authoritarian personality and anti-intellectualism has cast a shadow over the intellectual outlook of Negroes.

An Arena of Political Life

It was inevitable that preachers who had played such an important role in the organized social life of Negroes should become political leaders during the Reconstruction period when the Negro enjoyed civil rights.[28] The career of Bishop Henry M. Turner of the African Methodist Episcopal Church will enable us to see how these leaders in the religious life of Negroes became, after Emancipation, leaders in politics. He was born in South Carolina of free ancestry in 1834.[29] On his mother's side he was the grandson of an African prince. He was able to acquire some education through private instruction. When fourteen years of age he joined the Methodist Church and later became a chaplain in the United States Army. After the Civil War he transferred to the African Methodist Episcopal Church in which he advanced from a position of an itinerant preacher to that of an elder. During this time he became active in politics. He organized Negroes in the Republican Party in Georgia and was elected to the Georgia legislature. Turner was expelled from the Georgia legislature when white supremacy was restored in Georgia and as the result of persecution he was forced to resign as postmaster of Macon, Georgia, a position to which he had been appointed by President Grant. Turner abandoned politics and devoted his life to the church.

During the Reconstruction period a number of outstanding leaders in the Baptist and in the other Methodist denominations became outstanding as leaders of Negroes in politics. Bishop James W. Hood of the African Methodist Episcopal Zion Church was elected president of a convention of Negroes in North Carolina which was perhaps the first political convention called by Negroes after they gained their freedom. He served as a local magistrate and later as a Deputy Collector of Internal Revenue for the United States.[30] Hood was also appointed Assistant Superintendent of Public Instruction of the State of North Carolina. These ministers who became the political leaders of Negroes were all Republicans and shared on the whole the conservative political philosophy of the party.

It should be noted that the twenty Negroes elected to the House of Representatives of the United States from the South during the Reconstruction period only two were preachers, but one of the two Negroes who were elected to the Senate was a preacher.[31] Senator Hiram R. Revels, one of the two Negroes elected from Mississippi, was born a free Negro in North Carolina in 1822. He moved to the North and was ordained in the African Methodist Episcopal Church. When the Civil War broke out he assisted in organizing two Negro regiments in Maryland. He worked with the Freedmen's Bureau and, like other preachers, engaged in the establishment of churches and schools before entering politics in Mississippi. Revel's career in politics, like that of other Negro preachers, was of short duration because of the reestablishment of white supremacy in the South. After elimination from politics in the South, the Negro preachers generally devoted themselves to their church though in some cases they became heads of Negro schools.

As the result of the elimination of Negroes from the political life of the American community, the Negro church became the arena of their political activities. The church was the main area of social life in which Negroes could aspire to become the leaders of men. It was the area of social life where ambitious individuals could achieve distinction and the symbols of status. The church was the arena in which the struggle for power and the thirst for power could be satisfied. This was especially important to Negro men who had never been able to assert themselves and assume the dominant male role, even in family relations, as defined by American culture. In the Baptist churches, with their local autonomy, individual Negro preachers ruled their followers in an arbitrary manner, while the leaders in the hierarchy of the various Methodist denominations were czars, rewarding and punishing their subordinates on the basis of personal loyalties. Moreover, the monetary rewards which went with power were not small when one considers the contributions of millions of Negroes and the various business activities of the churches.

The Negro church was not only an arena of political life for the leaders of Negroes, it had a political meaning for the masses. Although they were denied the right to vote in the American community, within their churches, especially the Methodist Churches, they could vote and engage in electing their officers. The elections of bishops and other officers and representatives to conventions has been a serious activity for the masses of Negroes. But, in addition, the church had a political significance for Negroes in a broader meaning of the term. The development of the Negro church after Emancipation was tied up, as we have seen, largely with the Negro family. A study of Negro churches in a Black Belt county in Georgia in 1903 revealed, for example, that a large proportion of the churches were "family churches." [32] Outside of the family, the church represented the only other organized social existence. The rural Negro communities in the South were named after their churches. In fact, the Negro population in the rural South has been organized in "church communities" which represented their widest social orientation and the largest social groups in which they found an identification. Moreover, since the Negro was an outsider in the American community, it was the church that enlisted his deepest loyalties. Therefore, it was more than an amusing incident to note some years ago in a rural community in Alabama, that a Negro when asked to identify the people in the adjoining community replied: "The nationality in there is Methodist." We must remember that these people have no historic traditions and language and sentiments to identify them as the various nationalities of Europe. For the Negro masses, in their social and moral isolation in American society, the Negro church community has been a nation within a nation.

A Refuge in a Hostile White World

In providing a structured social life in which the Negro could give expression to his deepest feeling and at the same time achieve status and find a meaningful existence, the Negro church provided a refuge in a hostile white world. For the slaves who worked and suffered in an alien world, religion offered a means of catharsis for their pent-up emotions and frustrations. Moreover, it turned their minds from the sufferings and privations of this world to a world after death where the weary would find rest and the victims of injustices would be compensated. The Negroes who were free before the Civil War found status in the church which shielded them from the contempt and discriminations of the white world. Then for a few brief years after Emancipation the hopes and expectations of the black freedmen were raised and they thought that they would have acceptance and freedom in the white man's world. But their hopes and expectations were rudely shattered when white supremacy was reestablished in the South. They were excluded from participation in the white man's world except on the basis of inferiority. They were disfranchised and the public schools provided for them were a mere travesty on education. The courts set up one standard of justice for the white and another standard for the black man. They were stigmatized as an inferior race lacking even the human attributes which all men are supposed to possess. They were subjected to mob violence involving lynchings and burnings alive which were justified even by the white Christian churches.

Where could the Negro find a refuge from this hostile white world? They remembered from their Bible that the friends of Job had counselled him to curse God and die. They remembered too that Samson when blinded had torn down the Temple and destroyed himself along with his tormentors. Had not one of their leading ministers in his disillusionment and despair cried out against the flag of the nation he had served in the Civil War, "I don't want to die under the dirty rag." But the Negro masses did not curse God and die.[33] They could not pull down the Temple upon the white man and themselves.

They retained their faith in God and found a refuge in their churches.

The Negro church with its own forms of religious worship was a world which the white man did not invade but only regarded with an attitude of condescending amusement. The Negro church could enjoy this freedom so long as it offered no threat to the white man's dominance in both economic and social relations. And, on the whole, the Negro's church was not a threat to white domination and aided the Negro to become accommodated to an inferior status. The religion of the Negro continued to be other-worldly in its outlook, dismissing the privations and sufferings and injustices of this world as temporary and transient.[34] The Negro church remained a refuge despite the fact that the Negro often accepted the disparagement of Negroes by whites and the domination of whites.[35] But all of this was a part of God's plan and was regarded just as the physical environment was regarded. What mattered was the way he was treated in the church which gave him an opportunity for self-expression and status. Since the Negro was not completely insulated from the white world and had to conform to some extent to the ways of white men, he was affected by their evaluation of him. Nevertheless, he could always find an escape from such, often painful, experiences within the shelter of his church.

4

NEGRO RELIGION IN THE CITY

The Migration to Cities

THE migrations of Negroes to cities, especially to northern cities, produced a crisis in the life of the Negro similar in many respects to the crisis created by the Civil War and Emancipation. Immediately following Emancipation, Negroes drifted into the cities of the South in larger numbers proportionately than the whites. Then, after a decade or so, there was an almost imperceptible drift of the Negroes to hundreds of southern cities until the First World War when the mass migrations of Negroes to northern cities was set in motion. Until the First World War about nine-tenths of the Negroes were still in the South and about four-fifths of those in the South lived in rural areas. The War created an unprecedented demand on the part of northern industries for workers, especially large numbers of unskilled workers. The War had cut off the immigration of workers from Europe and many immigrant workers returned to Europe in order to fight for their homelands. The mass movement of Negroes from the South was stimulated also by floods and the ravages of the boll weevil as well as the oppression which Negroes had suffered. As the result of the mass movements from the South large Negro communities were created in the metropolitan areas of the North. Although the movements slowed down after the War, Negroes continued to migrate to the cities of the North and during the Second World War southern

Negroes were attracted by the war industries to the cities of the West. Negroes have continued to move into southern cities as well as into the cities of the North and West, with the result that nearly two-thirds of the Negroes in the country as a whole live under urban conditions.

The movement of Negroes to cities, we have said, created a crisis similar to that resulting from Emancipation. It was a crisis in that it uprooted the masses of Negroes from their customary way of life, destroying the social organization which represented both an accommodation to conditions in the rural South and an accommodation to their segregated and inferior status in southern society. In the city environment the family of the masses of Negroes from rural areas, which lacked an institutional basis and was held together only by cooperation in making a living or by sympathies and sentiments generated by living together in the same household, was unable to stand the shock of the disintegrating forces in urban life. Often men who went ahead to the cities with firm resolve to send for their wives and children acquired new interests and never sent for their families. Even when families migrated to the cities, they often disintegrated when they no longer had the support of friends and neighbors and the institutions which had held together families in the rural South. As a result there were many footloose men and homeless women in the cities who had broken all family ties. Moreover, since the women in families were required to work as well as the men, the children were no longer subject to family discipline. The disorganization of the Negro family in the city was reflected in the large numbers of women who had been deserted by their husbands, by the increased numbers of unmarried mothers, and by the high rate of juvenile delinquency among Negroes.

In the cold impersonal environment of the city, the institutions and associations which had provided security and support for the Negro in the rural environment could not be resurrected. The mutual aid or "sickness and burial" societies could no longer provide security during the two major crises which the Negroes feared most. In fact, in the crowded slums of northern cities, neighborliness and friendship no longer had any meaning. The Negro could not find even the warmth and sympathy of the secret fraternal organizations which had added color and ornament to a drab existence in the South.

The most important crisis in the life of the Negro migrant was produced by the absence of the church which had been the center of his social life and a refuge from a hostile white world. The Negro church, as we have seen, was not only the organization that had created cohesion among the slaves but it was also the basis of organized life among the Negroes who were free before the Civil War and among the freedmen following Emancipation. Moreover, it had set the pattern for organized social life among Negroes. We are interested in discovering how the breakdown of the traditional social organization of Negro life in the city resulted in the transformation of the Negro church and changed the religious behavior of Negroes.

The Secularization of the Churches

In the urban environment the entire mental outlook of Negroes was changed. This was especially true with the migrants who went to the large metropolitan centers and industrial cities of the North. In the strange environment the Negro endeavored to explain his new experiences in terms of his traditional outlook on life which was saturated with his religion and the image of the world provided by his knowledge of the Bible. This is shown vividly in the letters which the migrants sent home to their families, often through the pastor of the church to which they belonged in the South.[1] In one letter a migrant to Pittsburgh undertook to describe the marvel of the gigantic blazing steel furnaces by writing that they were just like what would happen on Judgment Day. But the new experiences could not be contained in the traditional ways of thinking about the world. Even the illiterate migrants could not remain unaffected by the new ideas and above all the new ways of behaving in the urban environment. They were impressed by the new status in which they found themselves. They marveled at the fact that their children went to school with white children and the white teachers addressed them as Mister and Mistress. They saw Negroes in unaccustomed roles as policemen and firemen and in positions of trust and authority and that Negroes could vote as white men did. Through these experiences they acquired a new conception of Negroes and of themselves.

The change in status was related in part to the fact that in the northern city the Negro children received the same education as the white child even when they were not in the same school with whites. The education was of a nature to broaden their intellectual horizon and give them an entirely new outlook on life. In addition, education opened the door to many occupations that had been closed to Negroes on account of race in the South. As a consequence there was an acceleration of the occupational differentiation of the Negro population in northern cities. Whereas, for example, preachers constituted about fifty percent of the professional class among Negroes in the South, in northern cities, where nearly nine-tenths of the Negroes in the North lived, only one professional Negro in ten was a preacher. And what was important, Negroes were not only to be found in most of the occupational groups in the northern cities but Negro professional men and women and white-collar workers were not confined to the Negro community as in the South.

On the basis of the occupational differentiation of the Negro population, a new system of social stratification or socio-economic classes came into existence. We have noted the simple stratification of the Negro community in the South which consisted of a small upper class based largely upon family and a light complexion and later based to some degree upon education. As a result of the entrance of Negroes into new occupations, some of whom served the new needs of the large Negro communities in northern cities, a new class structure emerged consisting of three major classes.[2] This new class system has not only helped to change the traditional organization of Negro life but it has caused the Negro church to adapt itself to the general outlook and religious requirements of the different classes.

From the standpoint of formal affiliation with the various denominations, it appears from available statistics that the Negro in the northern city continued his traditional affiliation. That is to say, nearly two-thirds of the Negroes continued to attend Baptist churches and about a third were in the various Methodist churches. Most of the remainder of the Negroes who were affiliated with the church were in the Episcopal and Presbyterian churches, and a small number in the Roman Catholic Church. But these figures fail to tell what had occurred in the Negro churches and in the religious behavior of Negroes. The change which occurred can be best described as a secularization of the Negro churches. By secularization we mean that the Negro churches lost their predominantly other-worldly outlook and began to focus attention upon the Negro's condition in this world. The most obvious evidence of secularization has been that the churches have been forced to tolerate card playing and dancing and theater-going. The opposition to these forms of recreation was rationalized on the basis that they would lead to gambling and immorality rather than that they were sinful.[3]

A more important indication of the growing secularization of Negro churches has been their interest in the affairs of the community.[4] The interest in the affairs of the community included recreational work and contributions to the work of a social welfare agency like the National Urban League or organizations fighting for civil rights like the National Association for the Advancement of Colored People. This new direction of interest in worldly affairs was more strongly indicated by the nature of the sermons of the ministers and their leadership in political affairs in which their church members actively participated.[5] In a number of nothern cities the pastors of large Negro churches have been influential in politics and have received important political appointments.[6] It is no accident that one of the four Negro members of the House of Representatives of the United States is a preacher, the Reverend Adam Clayton Powell, the pastor of the Abyssinian Baptist Church in New York City which is reported to be the largest church in the United States. Reverend Powell has not only been a political leader of Negroes but he has also marched with them in the boycott of stores which refused to employ Negroes.

The secularization of the Negro church has not affected to the same extent and in the same manner all sections of the Negro population. The manner in which secularization has affected Negroes is related to the new stratification of the Negro population. In a study of stratification in Negro churches in Chicago, it was found that church-going was not important for many persons of upper-class status and that those who attended church attended churches with services that were ritualistic and deliberative, the Episcopal, Presbyterian, and Congregational.[7] The upper middle class was found to be affiliated with the same churches as the upper class with the important difference, however, that the upper middle class was more faithful in church attendance. Some members of the upper middle class also attended the Methodist and Baptist churches for social reasons. On the other hand, the members of the lower middle class were affiliated with churches which were described as semidemonstrative, as there was emotional participation on the part of the members. This was indicative of their recent social ascension from the lower class for whom demonstrative participation in the church services is regarded as indispensable. In fact, some of the members of the lower middle class preferred to attend certain Methodist and Baptist churches for this very reason.

In the cities of the North the churches were much larger than the churches in the South. The average membership of a Negro church in the North was close to 800 while the average for the South was less than half that number.[8] The Negro preacher in the northern city has striven to build up large churches which are a measure of his status and influence, not to mention his control of economic resources. These churches are vast social organizations with a number of departments concerned with many aspects of Negro life other than the religious. They have established systems of bookkeeping and something approaching an impersonal bureaucratic organization. In spite of the wealth and power of these churches, they repel the Negro masses who seek a type of religious association that is warm and intimate and in which they have a satisfactory status.

Religion in the "Storefront" Church

The inadequacy, from a religious standpoint, of the institutional denominations accounts for the "storefront"
churches which one finds in Negro communities in American
cities. In the survey of Negro churches in twelve cities, to
which we have referred, out of a total of 2104 church buildings, 777 were "storefront" churches or houses and the
remainder were conventional church buildings.[9] These
"storefront" churches, as the name suggests, are generally
conducted in unrented or abandoned stores, though some
may be found in run-down houses. They are located in the
poorer and deteriorated areas of Negro communities. They
often owe their existence to the initiative on the part of a
"Jack-leg" preacher, that is, a semiliterate or an uneducated
preacher, who gathers about him the poorer Negroes who
seek a religious leader in the city. Nearly a half of 777
"storefront" churches in the study referred to above were
Baptist and a somewhat smaller number were known as
Holiness and Spiritualist churches. There were less than ten
churches identified with any of the three regularly established
Methodist denominations though many of the members of
these "storefront" churches had been in Methodist churches.

The "storefront" church represents an attempt on the part
of the migrants, especially from the rural areas of the South,
to reestablish a type of church in the urban environment to
which they were accustomed. They want a church, first of all,
in which they are known as people. In the large city church
they lose their identity completely and, as many of the
migrants from the rural South have said, neither the church
members nor the pastor knows them personally. Sometimes
they complain with bitterness that the pastor of the large city
church knows them only as the number on the envelope in
which they place their dues. In wanting to be treated as
human beings, they want status in the church which was the
main or only organization in the South in which they had
status. Some of the statements concerning their reason for
leaving the big denominational churches was that "back
home in the South" they had a seat in the church that
everyone recognized as theirs and that if the seat were empty

on Sunday the pastor came to their homes to find out the cause of their absence.

The desire for the warm and intimate association of fellow worshippers in church services was not the only reason why the "storefront" church was more congenial to the recently urbanized Negro than the cold impersonal atmosphere of the large denominational city church. In these small "storefront" churches the Negro migrant could worship in a manner to which he had been accustomed. The sermon by the pastor is of a type to appeal to traditional ideas concerning hell and heaven and the imagery which the Negro has acquired from the Bible. Much emphasis is placed upon sins of the flesh, especially sexual sins. The preacher leads the singing of the Spirituals and other hymns with which the Negroes with a folk background are acquainted. The singing is accompanied by "shouting" or holy dancing which permits the maximum of free religious expression on the part of the participants.

In the cities of the North and even in the cities in the South, these "storefront" churches are constantly being organized by all kinds of so-called preachers in order to attract lower-class Negroes. During the 1920s when southern Negroes were flocking to Harlem in New York City, it was found that only 54 out of 140 churches in Harlem were housed in regular church structures.[10] The remainder were of the "storefront" type which had been organized by preachers, many of whom were exploiters and charlatans. They based their appeal on the Negro's desire to find salvation in the next world and to escape from sickness and the insecurities of this world. One of these churches advertised:

> We Believe that all Manner of Disease Can Be Cured
> Jesus is the Doctor
> Services on Sunday.[11]

The large number of churches in Negro communities in the North as well as in the South has raised the question as to whether the Negro population is over-churched.[12] There is no way of answering this question, and it is irrelevant in a sense when one considers the important role of the Negro church in the organization of the Negro community. The vast majority of

Negroes have constituted a lower class, gaining a living as common laborers and in domestic and personal service. Among these people there is little associational life and the churches of all types represent, as we have seen, the main form of organized social life. Even when Negroes have broken away from the traditional churches they have sought in new religious groups a way of life which would conform to their needs. This may be seen when we turn to consider the cults which have grown up in recent years among Negroes.

Negro Cults in the City

The cults which have developed among Negroes represent something new in the religious life of Negroes. They are sometimes not differentiated from the traditional religious groups which meet in abandoned stores and houses because the cults often meet in the same type of buildings. In most of the "storefront" churches the Negro maintains his traditional beliefs and conceptions of God and the world and himself. On the other hand, in the new cults which flourish in the cities, Negroes have abandoned their traditional notions about God and the world and, what is of crucial importance, their conceptions of themselves. An attempt has been made to classify the different types of cults from the standpoint of such features as faith healing or holiness or whether they claim an Islamic origin,[13] but there is much overlapping. Moreover, while all these cults represent "New Gods of the City," [14] there is an important difference between those which seek to restore a purer form of Christianity or sanctification and holiness and those which tend to be secular in outlook and represent primarily a complete transformation of the Negro as a race. Of course, in some of those cults in which the Negro escapes from his racial identity, there may be faith healing and sanctification, but these are subordinate to the main orientation of the cults.

We shall begin with the cults which seek to restore a purer form of Christianity through the sanctification of their members. In Chicago, 107 of the 475 churches were Holiness churches and 51 Spiritualist.[15] The Holiness churches are composed of people who seek to restore the church as it was given to the Saints. The chief religious activity of the members of the Holiness cults is that form of ecstatic worship which is known as "getting happy" or "shouting." This frenzied behavior is often accompanied by drums, guitars, or tambourines. The worship in these Holiness churches is the type of behavior which Daniel studied in the nine ecstatic cults.[16] They insist that Christians shall live free of sin and in a state of holiness. They refuse to compromise with the sinful ways of the world. By sin they mean the use of tobacco, the drinking of alcoholic beverages, cursing and swearing, dancing, playing cards, and adultery. All of such activities are regarded as "carnal-mindedness." [17] In recounting their achievement of a state of holiness, some members tell of having visions of heaven. They claim, as a pastor of a Holiness church said, that they "are the common ordinary people that Jesus dwelt among." [18]

One of these Holiness churches in Philadelphia was founded by a woman, known as Bishop Ida Robinson, who was born in Florida and grew up in Georgia.[19] She was converted at the age of seventeen and became active in the church. However, she left the South and went to Philadelphia where she founded the Mt. Sinai Holy Church in 1924. Bishop Robinson is described as "tall, sharp of feature and eye, medium brown in color, probably of mixed Indian-Negro blood. Her education has been limited, but she is extremely intelligent, and a competent leader. She is, of course, a keen student of the Bible." [20] She acquired the building for her church from a white Pentecostal congregation. She is the supreme head of the cult because, as she claims, her authority comes directly from God. She has ordained a woman as vice-bishop and a number of elders and preachers who are heads of member churches in other cities.

Membership in this church is determined by a period of testing which "is known as sanctification, and an experience, usually speaking in tongues, which is the sign that one has been filled with the Holy Spirit." [21] After one becomes a member one may join the Preachers' Class in which one is drilled in the Bible and "spiritual wisdom." Financial support of the church is provided through tithes and collections taken at the services when the bishop leads the members to the collection table. At these services there is singing and the clapping of hands after which there are testimonies. These testimonies tell of God's having guided these witnesses to the power of Holy Spirit in healing ills of the body. The sermon by the bishop which consists of attacks upon the sins of the world, which is approaching its end, results in the rising of individuals who become frenzied as they speak in tongues and engage in "shouting." After the bishop leaves or rests, there are other services which culminate in a communion service during which they drink grape juice and are served crackers. The practices of the church include the tabooing of divorce and marriage outside the circle of members. Men and women may show sentiment toward each other only when they plan to marry. Women are required to dress in a "holy" manner which means wearing plain black or white dresses and stockings, preferably of cotton, and if men wear neckties they must be plain white or black.

The most important and most widely known of the Holiness cults is the Father Divine Peace Mission Movement.[22] Little is known of the history of Father Divine before 1919, when he acquired a modest cottage in Sayville, New Jersey, in response to an advertisement that one or two German-Americans, who still continued to fight the Great War, would sell even to "colored buyers." Major J. Divine, as he signed his name, and "Pinninah," his wife, opened a free employment bureau but soon began to take in the destitute and feed them. During the next ten years or so people flocked in increasing numbers to the house for religious services and "Reverend" Divine became "Father" Divine. He added rooms to the house, which began to be known as "Heaven," as the number of people came to "lift their voices in praise of Father Divine." The visitors were impressed by the sumptuous feasts which were served after Father Divine had blessed every dish. Legends began to grow concerning the unlimited wealth of Father Divine and his miraculous powers of healing. Those who listened at the shaded windows "were shocked by ejaculations in which rapture and pain were intermingled with cries of 'Thank you, Father.' "[23]

It was not long before the attention of the public authorities was called to the fact that women were living in the "Heaven." Moreover, the white residents complained about the noise and the motley throng of men and women who were attracted to these emotional orgies. Divine became a sort of martyr when he and his followers were arrested and he was indicted for maintaining a public nuisance. When Divine refused to cooperate with authorities his case was taken before Justice Lewis J. Smith of the Supreme Court of Nassau County, a Presbyterian who was disgusted that educated white men and women should testify that they believed Divine was the "personified perfection" of God. Divine was found guilty by a jury and sentenced to jail. Within less than a week after Divine's conviction, Justice Smith died unexpectedly. It was this event that set on Father Divine the seal of omnipotence in the eyes of his followers. Divine was released from jail on bail during an appeal to the Appellate Court which reversed the ruling of Judge Smith. In Harlem at a mass meeting characterized by shouting and singing where white women as well as black sought to kiss his hand there occurred "the apotheosis, the deification of the man who acclaimed himself Father Divine." [24]

Father Divine's Peace Mission Movement is distinguished from other cults first by the fact that Father Divine is the organization and that all directions are issued by him. This follows logically from the fact that Father Divine is God.[25] He is surrounded by secretaries, the majority of whom are white and Negro women, who record everything he says and transmit his orders to his followers. His intimate participation in every activity is indicated by his role at the banquet table or Holy Communion, where every dish passes through his hands, he pours the first glass of water, cuts the first slice of cake, and places the serving spoon in each container. Certain figures are close to Divine, one being his personal secretary and the other his wife, known as Mother Divine. Everything done, even in other cities, must meet with his approval and he meets scores of his followers daily from far and near. His followers have been estimated from thousands to several millions but nobody knows the actual number. Nor is it easy to ascertain how membership is attained. It appears that one type of member is the person who subscribes to the beliefs and practices and attends service and the other has renounced the world completely and joins the "kingdom" after disposing of his

worldly goods according to instructions. He becomes completely subject to the will of Father Divine. This is all tied up
with the question of the support of the movement, a question
which no one has been able to answer.[26]

Another important feature of this cult is that it does not
tolerate any form of racial discrimination. Wherever Negroes
and whites live together, they are required to eat and sleep
together.[27] This may account for the fact that the movement
has not spread into the South. At the same time it has been
suggested that the strict sexual taboos are designed to meet the
eventuality that the movement may spread into the South.
Nevertheless, after Mother Divine died, Father Divine married
a young white woman about twenty-two years of age, who has
become the new Mother Divine. The sex taboo forbids man
and wife to live together. When a married couple enter the cult,
they become brother and sister and can have no relations with
the opposite sex. Even dancing with members of the opposite sex
is forbidden.

Although intoxicants are strictly forbidden, there are no
food taboos. And what is more important, business enterprises
are encouraged. In fact, the movement publishes a weekly
periodical, *New Day,* which is the sacred text of the organization rather than the Bible. Father Divine discourages the
reading of the Bible. *New Day* contains every speech uttered by
Father Divine. It also carries advertisements of many large and
well-known commercial enterprises. Every advertisement
carries within its text the injunction: "Peace" and sometimes
adds "Thank you, Father." The use of such words as Negro and
white is forbidden. A single copy of *New Day* may contain 132
pages filled, with the exception of the advertisements, with the
words and activities of Father Divine.

The followers of Father Divine believe that he is God and
that he will never die. To them God has appeared as a Negro
because the Negro is the lowliest of God's creatures and God
prefers to bring salvation to the lowly. The followers of Father
Divine are not to refer to the passage of time, as for example,
age. A true follower of Father Divine will never die and illness
means that he has strayed from the faith. Death represents the
culmination of the failure to live according to the faith. When

faced with difficulty, the faithful need only to say, "Thank you, Father."

Father Divine made his triumphant entrance into Harlem during the first half of 1932 at the depth of the Great Depression. To hungry Harlem, "The real God is the God who feeds us." [28] Ten years later, Father Divine, though God, fled from New York City to Philadelphia in order to avoid a number of embarrassing lawsuits. There ensued a struggle for the spiritual control of the Negro masses in Harlem.[29] The two contenders were Elder Lightfoot Solomon Michaux, a former fish peddler, whose disciples call him the "Happy Am I Prophet," and the other was Mother Rosa Artimus Horne, a former seamstress, described as the "Pray for Me Priestess." One investigator has written as follows: "While sharing a mutual dislike for each other, the two oracles have many things in common. Both operate five temples throughout the nation; claim to be miraculous healers; profess national radio and sawdust trail followings numbering in the hundreds of thousands; are coy about revealing the exact amount of their earnings; and both are adroit showmen who harbor contempt for the methods of Father Divine." [30] Elder Michaux has a larger popular appeal and has been able to enhance his prestige by association with important public leaders. He has had mass baptisms in the Griffith Stadium in Washington, where two hundred white-robed candidates are immersed in water from the Potomac River. His sermons consist chiefly of tirades against sin, rowdy women, slot machines, whisky, beer, and gamblers. He is reputed to be a millionaire and keeps a retinue of servants, including cooks, valets, maids for his wife, and chauffeurs to drive his eight large automobiles. He has much influence among some government officials who regard him as a spokesman for many Negro church people.

Mother Horne, who lacked the humor of Elder Michaux, carried on a grim evangelism of the fire and brimstone variety.[31] She claimed to have raised thousands of people from the dead besides having made hundreds of the blind see. In their religious services the members of Mother Horne's cult are stimulated by clapping their hands to maddening rhythms accompanied by a piano and a drum. They generally give testimonies to the powers of Mother Horne while she illuminates these testimonies with such remarks as "punching the devil in the eye." She was reputed to have had properties worth millions of dollars which enabled her and her daughter to live well.

The recent death in 1960 of Bishop Charles Emmanuel Grace, better known as "Daddy" Grace, has brought to the attention of the American people a cult leader of considerable influence who possessed a considerable fortune. He was a man of mixed parentage, Negro and Portuguese, who came to the United States around 1920. He is said to have worked as a cook in the railway service before he began to preach in 1925.[32] He founded an organization known as the United House of Prayer for All People with churches in twenty or more cities along the eastern seaboard. Bishop Grace, with his flowing hair, was the undisputed head of the United House of Prayer. All monies had to be returned to Grace in his office in Washington. Membership in this organization was supposed to be based upon a special religious experience, but membership seemed to be open to anyone. There was considerable emphasis upon the money with the result that numerous collections were taken during the services. This cult is essentially a sect of the holiness type, including conversion, sanctification, and the usual taboos. According to Fauset, "the beliefs boil down to a worship of Daddy Grace. God appears to be all but forgotten."[33] Bishop Grace has been heard to tell his worshippers: "Never mind about God. Salvation is by Grace only. Grace has given God a vacation, and since God is on His vacation, don't worry Him. . . . If you sin against God, Grace can save you, but if you sin against Grace, God cannot save you."[34]

This cult is distinguished by physical frenzy in which the sex motive is prominent. With aid of a piano and a drum the worshippers engage in ecstatic dancing during which in response to allusions to sex motives, the worshippers cry out, "Daddy, you feel so good." These emotional debauches are generally used to collect money from the members. Moreover, Grace engaged in all kinds of businesses, the products of which bore his name, as for example, Daddy Grace Toothpaste.

When Bishop Grace died his wealth was variously estimated to be from five million to twenty-five million dollars. Since he died suddenly on the West Coast, the funeral *cortège* crossed the country, stopping at a number of cities for funeral services which provided occasions for wild frenzied gatherings on the part of his worshippers. He was finally buried in a large expensive mausoleum in New Bedford, Massachusetts, the scene of his first home in the United States.

Only relatively brief attention can be given to those cults which belong more specifically to the Spiritualistic group. It seems that the Spiritualist cult in Chicago was founded in New Orleans and transplanted to the North.[35] This cult flourished especially during the Great Depression. It should be noted that it borrowed its hymns from the Baptists and Methodists, and its altar candles and statues from the Catholic Church. The preachers and mediums wore colorful robes and offered healing advice, and "good luck" for a prayer and the price of a candle or holy flower. The mediums claimed direct contact with the sources of wisdom. The Spiritualist cult was differentiated from the Holiness cult by the fact that the former was not opposed to card-playing, dancing, or "sporting life." It was rumored that it might give advice in playing the illicit lottery game, known as "policy" or "the numbers."

We come finally to two cults which are of considerable importance because in them the Negro does not seek salvation in the usual sense but finds an escape from his identification as a Negro. One of these cults is the Church of God or Black Jews.[36] The cult was founded years ago by a Negro, known as Prophet F. S. Cherry, from "the Deep South, which he refers to as a place worse than hell." He is a self-educated man who has traveled over the world as a seaman and worked as a common laborer all over the United States. Prophet Cherry welcomes educated men to his church but takes a special pleasure in ridiculing educated people and making fun of their manners and ways of thinking. He seems to get a great deal of pleasure from his vituperations against the clergy whom he calls "damn fools" and "vultures." On his pulpit there is always a Bible in Yiddish and another in Hebrew, since he is conversant with these two languages. He does not wear a special dress as the leaders of many cults, except occasionally when he appears in a black academic gown, the sleeves having yellow stripes.

As the head of the cult Prophet Cherry appoints elders, who

may take his place in the pulpit, deacons, deaconesses, and secretaries who supervise the finances and the routine affairs of the organization. Membership in the organization is open to any "black" person. While it is highly desirable that new members should have a religious experience involving a vision or some kind of "spirit possession," this is not a requisite for membership. This cult looks with disfavor on "speaking in tongues" and emotion, though holy dancing within decent limitations is regarded as proper. There is no collection of money during services though there is a receptacle hanging at the door for donations as people enter the church and members are required to pay tithes.

The sacred text of the cult is really the Talmud instead of the Bible, but the prophet always refers to the Hebrew Bible as the final authority. The members of the cult think of themselves as Black Jews and insist that the so-called Jew is a fraud. They believe in Jesus Christ but claim that he was a black man. According to them the Black People were the original inhabitants of the earth. Moreover, God is black and Jacob was black. The enslavement of the Negro and his emancipation were foretold in the Bible and the world will never be right until Black Jews occupy high places in the world. Such beliefs provide the basis of the sermons by the Prophet. After the Italians invaded Ethiopia,[37] he railed against the Pope for condoning the invasion and predicted that Hitler would drive him out of Rome. Services are held on Sunday, Wednesday, and Friday evenings and all day Saturday, which is regarded as the Sabbath or Holy Day. The members of the cult do not observe Christmas or Easter. Funerals are to be held in funeral parlors and the deceased, who can only be viewed by very close relatives, must be taken from the house as soon as possible.

In this cult, it will be noted, the Negro members have found an escape from their traditional identification and lowly status and become the first people of the earth. Even God has become black. This transformation of the Negroes is reinforced by the learning of the Hebrew language on the part of the members of the cult. The fact that they have dispensed with the Bible as the final authority and refused to observe such Christian holidays as Christmas and Easter is an indication of the extent to which they have broken with traditional Negro religion. It is also significant that death and funerals, which have been such an important part of the religious life of the Negro, are of little consequence.

The second cult, the Moorish Science Temple of America, represents an even more radical departure from the traditional religion of the Negro. Moreover, as we shall see, it takes on the character of a nationalistic religion. The founder of the Moorish Science Temple was Timothy Drew, who was born in North Carolina in 1886.[38] Sometime in his life he came into contact with Oriental philosophy and "was impressed with its racial catholicity. The fruits of his research have been compressed into the Holy Koran of the Moorish Holy Temple of Science, which is not to be confused with the orthodox Mohammedan Koran." [39] Moreover, he became obsessed with the idea that Negroes could find salvation by discovering their national origin and refuse henceforth "to be called Negroes, black folk, colored people, or Ethiopians" and call themselves Asiatics or specifically Moors or Moorish Americans. He began his crusade by haranguing small groups of Negroes on street corners, in tenements, and on vacant lots. To compensate for his little formal education, he possessed a certain personal magnetism and gave evidence of being sincere in his desire to help Negroes to escape from race prejudice and racial discriminations. He established his first temple in Newark, New Jersey, and as his following increased, temples were set up in Pittsburgh, Detroit, and cities in the South. But his major achievement was the establishment of a temple in Chicago.

Hundreds of Negroes in Chicago flocked to the new leader, who had become known as Noble Drew Ali. They believed that the change in identification from Negro to Asiatic would bring salvation. The members were given a large calling card which bore the inscription: a replica of star and crescent with ISLAM beneath it, a replica of clasped hands with UNITY above it, and a replica of circled "7" with ALLAH beneath it.[40] Beneath this was the statement that the card represented their nationality and identification card, that the cult honored all divine prophets, Jesus, Mohammed, Buddah, and Confucius, and that the bearer was a Moslem under the Divine laws of the Holy Koran of Mecca, Love, Truth, Peace, Freedom, and Justice. There was added: "I AM A CITIZEN OF THE U.S.A."

Negroes who carried this card believed that the mere showing of the card would restrain white men if they would be inclined to disturb or harm Negroes. In fact, the members of the cult became so aggressive and insulting in their behavior toward whites, that it was necessary for the Noble Drew Ali to admonish them against such behavior. As the cult grew, some Negroes with education joined the organization and attempted to exploit the members by selling "herbs, magical charms, and potions, and literature pertaining to the cult." As the internal strife increased, one of these would-be leaders was killed, and Noble Drew Ali was arrested for murder, though he was not in Chicago at the time. He died under mysterious circumstances after being released from jail under bond and was awaiting trial. After the death of Noble Drew Ali, the cult split into a number of sects with some claiming that they were following him in his reincarnation.

Something needs to be said about the beliefs and ritual and practices of the cult. The members of the various sects which have split off from the parent body live according to the teachings which have been divulged to Noble Drew Ali and are contained in the Holy Koran.[41] Jesus figures largely in the Koran but Allah is God and He ordained his Prophet, Noble Drew Ali, to divulge his secrets to the dark folk of America. The charter of the Moorish Science Temple is supposed to have come from the "great capital empire of Egypt." Negro (black) signifies death and colored something painted. Therefore, the term "Moorish-American" must be used. In their religious services, which meet promptly and are dismissed promptly, the contents of the Holy Koran are expounded to the members. During the services, which are extremely quiet, men and women are segregated. " 'Christmas' is observed on January fifth, the anniversary of the day when the prophet, Noble Drew Ali, was reincarnated." Members greet each other, the right hand upraised and the palm turned out, with the words "Peace" and "Islam." There are a number of taboos, including the prohibition of the use of meat and eggs, the use of intoxicants, attendance at European games, and the straightening of the hair.

The Moorish Science Temple represents the most radical secularization of Negro religion or of the Negro church in the city. While the regular denominations have increasingly focused attention upon the solution of the Negro's problems or his salvation in this world, they have the essentials of traditional Negro religion. Likewise, in the "storefront" churches, there is an attempt among the lower class to re-create in the urban environment a type of religious organization in which they can find warm and sympathetic association and status. In a sense these changes in the traditional religious life of the Negro are an attempt to escape from the hard conditions under which Negroes live in the cities and to find a meaning for living. This escape is most marked in those cults in which the Negro becomes a new person, as in the cult of the Black Jews and the Moorish Science Temple. This latter cult is especially important both because it provides the Negro with a kind of national identification and because of its extremely secular outlook. This secular outlook is becoming common among the masses who are without church affiliation and scorn the saying which was once popular among the humble masses: "Take the world and give me Jesus." It is also evident among those who though still affiliated with churches do not trust to the Providence of God alone, but hope that the "numbers," or chance, will bring them security or fortune. Among those who depend upon chance there are many who have a purely hedonistic outlook on life and organize their lives around "good-timing." But most of them aspire to middle-class ideals and want to "get ahead." All of this is the result of the uprooting of the Negro from his traditional social organization in which the Negro church was the most important institution and set the patterns of behavior and thought and the values for the majority of Negroes.

5

THE NEGRO CHURCH AND ASSIMILATION

The Walls Came Tumbling Down

In the last chapter we have studied the transformations which have occurred in the Negro church and in the religion of Negroes as the result of urbanization. We have seen how the migrations of Negroes to cities have tended to uproot the traditional organization of the Negro community and changed the outlook of Negroes. As the result of the social disorganization of Negro life there has been a reorganization of life on a different basis in order to meet the demands of the city. Life in the cities of the North has brought a larger measure of freedom from racial prejudice and discriminations which had characterized race relations in the South. This new freedom has enabled Negroes to enter more into the mainstream of American life. Since this new freedom has been due partly to broad changes in the economic and social organization of American life, the Negro in the South benefited from these changes. The success which Negroes have achieved in breaking down racial barriers has been due partly to their own efforts. They have carried on a constant struggle in the courts and they have influenced to some extent public opinion. As the mid-century drew to a close a distinguished white woman, who had been associated with their struggle, could look back at the success which Negroes had made in breaking through racial barriers and say in the words of the well-known Negro spiritual, "the walls came tumbling down." [1]

However, as the racial barriers are broken down and Negroes increasingly enter into the mainstream of American life, the traditional organization of Negro life is constantly being undermined. The so-called process of integration, which is only an initial stage in the assimilation of Negroes into American society, does not have the same effect on all parts of the social structure of the Negro community. The extent and the nature of the participation of Negroes in the wider American community is determined first by their class position. Negroes in the Black Belt or rural counties in the South where they constitute 50 percent or more of the population are still almost completely isolated from the main currents of American culture. Although lower-class Negroes in cities, who include those engaged in domestic and personal services and those employed as unskilled laborers, have more contacts with American life, they are still more or less confined to the Negro community. As Negro workers acquire skills and become members of labor unions, they begin to enter into the mainstream of American life. This is, of course, more characteristic of Negro workers in the North than of those in the South. Many Negroes in the North who are employed as white-collar workers and in technical and professional occupations enter even more fully into the main currents of American society. Not only does their work enable them to share more fully in American culture but they associate more freely with their white fellow workers than any other section of the Negro population.

The second factor and a factor of equal importance, which determines the nature and extent of the participation of Negroes in the wider American community, is their own institutional life. The system of racial segregation in the United States has resulted in an almost complete duplication of the institutions of the American community within the Negro community.[2] We shall begin by considering those institutions which embody the secular interests of Negroes. As Negroes have moved from the world of the folk, they have established insurance companies and banks which have a purely secular end. These institutions are becoming a part of the different associations of insurance companies and banks and they are subject to state supervision. Then there are many other kinds of business enterprises, many of which cater especially to the personal and other needs of Negroes, and thus supply services often refused by white establishments. Negroes are expected to patronize these various so-called Negro businesses because of "racial loyalty." There is a National Negro Business League and numerous Negro chambers of commerce. Among the more successful Negro businesses should be included the Negro weekly newspapers which have circulations running into the hundreds of thousands.

Then there are certain cultural institutions among which are included the various secret fraternal organizations such as the Masons, Odd Fellows, and the Elks. In this group we would also include the various college Greek letter societies for men and women. Although they would not qualify as institutions, there are numerous social clubs which may be considered along with the cultural institutions. The most important cultural institution is, of course, the Negro church. It embodies, as we have seen, the cultural traditions of Negroes to a far greater extent than any other institution.

As "the walls of segregation tumble down," it is the institutions which embody the secular interests of Negroes which are being undermined more rapidly than those representing their cultural interests. As white establishments cater to the personal needs of Negroes there is less need for what is known as "Negro" businesses to supply such services. Moreover, as the large corporations and other so-called white business enterprises employ Negroes in all capacities, there is less need for an association of people engaged in "Negro" businesses. Likewise, as white newspapers carry more news concerning Negroes and employ Negro journalists, the Negro newspapers decline in circulation as the foreign language newspapers have done. Although schools are cultural institutions, the segregated Negro public schools and state colleges will become less important.

The situation is different in regard to the cultural institutions within the Negro community. There are some privately supported Negro educational institutions with deeply rooted traditions in Negro life that resist the trend toward the integration of the Negro. On the other hand, as Negro professors are increasingly taken on the faculties of so-called white colleges and universities and Negro students are admitted to such institutions, Negroes are joining the mainstream of American life. When one comes to the Negro church which is the most important cultural institution created by Negroes, one encounters the most important institutional barrier to integration and the assimilation of Negroes. White churches may open their doors to Negroes and a few Negro ministers may be invited to become pastors of white churches; the masses of Negroes continue, nevertheless, to attend the Negro churches and the Negro church as an institution continues to function as an important element in the organized social life of Negroes.

The Church Is No Longer a Refuge

The strength of the Negro church as a barrier to the integration of Negroes into the main currents of American life should not be overestimated, especially since the process of integration has not progressed very far. Moreover, it is necessary to differentiate the situation in the North from that in the South. In the South the Negro has scarcely begun his struggle to participate in the secular and public institutions of the American community. On the other hand, in the border states and in the North there is much larger participation of Negroes in the secular and public institutions of the American community. In the South the lives of Negroes still revolve about the activities of the Negro community. Even where they gain entrance into labor unions, they are excluded from the "social" activities of these organizations. In the North Negroes are included increasingly in the "social" activities of the various labor unions. Nevertheless, in the North the proliferation of organizations which provide for the "social" needs of Negroes indicates the extent to which Negroes are still outsiders, so to speak. Moreover, the ecological or spatial segregation of Negroes, which is often the result of impersonal economic and social forces rather than prejudice and discrimination, tends to maintain the separate institutions of the Negro community. The church is the most important of these institutions in which the masses of Negroes find a refuge within white society which treats them with condescension if not contempt.

But the Negro church can no longer serve as a refuge as it did in the past when the majority of Negroes lived in the South under a system of racial segregation and the majority of the Negroes in the South lived in rural areas. Willy-nilly, Negroes are drawn into the complex social organization of the American community. This is necessary for mere survival. Recognizing the need for a more complex social organization to serve the needs of urbanized Negroes and at the same time taking cognizance of the fact that Negroes were still excluded from labor unions, a Negro sociologist proposed that the Negro church, being the largest organized unit of Negro life, incorporate some of the functions of the new forms of organized social life which are required in the city.[3] It is apparent, however, that this proposal was impractical since the Negro church could not perform the functions of the new types of associations necessary to life in the city.

It was inevitable that the Negro should be drawn into the organized forms of social life in the urban environment. As a consequence, the Negro church has lost much of its influence as an agency of social control. Its supervision over the marital and family life of Negroes has declined. The church has ceased to be the chief means of economic cooperation. New avenues have been opened to all kinds of business ventures in which secular ends and values are dominant. The church is no longer the main arena for political activities which was the case when Negroes were disfranchised in the South. Negro political leaders have to compete with the white political leaders in the "machine" politics of the cities. In a word, the Negroes have been forced into competition with whites in most areas of social life and their church can no longer serve as a refuge within the American community.

We have seen how Negroes in the established denominational churches developed secular interests in order to deal with race prejudice and discriminations to which they are exposed when the "walls of segregation come tumbling down." We have seen how lower-class Negroes have reacted to the cold impersonal environment of the city and of the large denominational churches by joining the "storefront" churches and the various cults. These all represented their reaction to the crumbling traditional organization of Negro life as Negroes are increasingly cast afloat in the mainstream of American life, where they are still outsiders.

The Gospel Singers

Although the lower strata in the Negro community do not participate to the same extent as the upper strata in the main currents of American life, they are nevertheless increasingly assimilating the manners and customs of American society. There is thus achieved a certain external conformity to the patterns of American culture.[4] They continue to be influenced in their thinking and especially in their feelings and sentiments by the social heritage of the Negro which is represented by the Spirituals and religious orientation toward the world contained in the Spirituals. The masses of Negroes may increasingly criticize the church and their ministers, but they cannot escape from their heritage. They may develop a more secular outlook on life and complain that the church and the ministers are not sufficiently concerned with the problems of the Negro race,[5] yet they find in their religious heritage an opportunity to satisfy their deepest emotional yearnings.

Out of the revolt of the lower strata against the church and the growing secularization of Negro religion there has come an accommodation between traditional Negro religion and the new outlook of Negroes in the new American environment. This accommodation is symbolized by the Gospel Singers. The songs which the Gospel Singers sing have been described as a compound of "elements found in the old tabernacle songs, the Negro Spirituals and the blues." [6] Since the Negro has become urbanized, there has been an amazing rise and spread of "gospel singing." This has been attributed, and correctly so, to the fact that, "As Negro churches have become more European in decorum and program, the great mass of less Europeanized Negroes began to look elsewhere for full vented religious expressions in music and preaching." [7] The important fact is that although the Gospel

Singers have gone outside the church for a congenial form of religious expression, they nevertheless remain in the church and are a part of the church. Recently when a Gospel Singer died and her funeral was held in a large Baptist church in the nation's capital, it was reported that 13,000 persons viewed her remains, a thousand persons jammed the church, and another thousand lined the sidewalks outside the church. Dozens of gospel-singing groups came from neighboring areas and as far away as Pennsylvania and Illinois. The white owner of a broadcasting company flew from Ohio to attend the funeral. Between 150 and 200 cars accompanied the body to the cemetery.[8]

More important still for us here is the fact that the Gospel Singers symbolize something that is characteristic of Negro religion from the standpoint of assimilation. Some of the so-called advanced Negro churches resented these Gospel Singers and refused to permit them to sing within their churches. They have gradually become more tolerant and let down the bars as the Gospel Singers have acquired status and acceptance within the white world. Such well-known gospel singers as Mahalia Jackson, Rosetta Thorpe, and the Ward Singers have been accepted as "artists." The Gospel Singer not only sings to the Negro world but sings to the white world. One of the famous Ward Sisters stated that the gospel singing is popular because ". . . it fills a vacuum in people's lives. For people who work hard and make little money it offers a promise that things will be better in the life to come."[9] She was thinking, of course, of Negroes but the Gospel Singers sing to white America as well. This is indicated by their hold on the record industry and their popularity on radio and television programs.

Gospel singing has, of course, became commercialized and that is another indication of the relation of Negro religious life to assimilation. It indicates in a sense the terms on which the Negro is being assimilated. Moreover, white men in the South are beginning to imitate the Negro Gospel Singers. And Negro gospel singing is often featured as a part of the programs on television. Thus, the religious folk songs of the Negro are becoming secularized despite the fact that the singing of them in secular entertainment is a concession to the so-called religious revival in the United States. The Gospel Singers, then, unlike the cults, do not represent a complete break with the religious traditions of the Negro. They represent or symbolize the attempt of the Negro to utilize his religious heritage in order to come to terms with changes in his own institutions as well as the problems of the world of which he is a part.

In a sense, therefore, the attempts of the Negro to resist segregation in the sit-down strikes in the South represent the same falling back upon his religious heritage in time of crisis. This movement on the part of Negro students in the South is supposed to be based upon the nonviolent resistance movement of Gandhi.[10] Some of its intellectual leaders like the Reverend Martin Luther King may use Gandhi's nonviolent resistance as an ideological justification of the movement, but Gandhism as a philosophy and a way of life is completely alien to the Negro and has nothing in common with the social heritage of the Negro. As Negro students go forth singing the Spirituals or the Gospel hymns when they engage in sit-down strikes or sing their Gospel songs in response to violence, they are behaving in accordance with the religious heritage of the Negro.

Then there is another aspect of this movement which needs to be considered in relation to the changes in the religion of the Negro. Because of the improvement in their economic conditions, an increasing number of Negro students are able to attend the colleges for Negroes in the South. They are being drawn from those strata in the Negro population closest to the rural background and who, therefore, are closest to the folk heritage of the Negro. Education, or more specially the opportunity to attend college, is the most important factor enabling Negroes to achieve middle-class status. Moreover, the leaders of this movement have seen something of the world because of their army or other experiences, or their parents have had similar experiences. In their revolt against the racial discrimination they must fall back upon the only vital social heritage that has meaning for them and that social heritage is the religious heritage represented by the Spirituals which are becoming secularized.

The Religion of the New Middle Class

We have already seen in the last chapter how the Negro church and Negro religion have been affected by the new class structure which is emerging among Negroes in cities, especially in the North. Here we are interested in the religious outlook of the new Negro middle class which has become important among Negroes during the past twenty years or so. It is this class whose outward appearance and standards of behavior approximate most nearly the norms of the white American society. Moreover, Negroes who have achieved middle-class status participate more largely than any other element in American life. It is for this reason that we shall focus attention upon the new middle class in studying the changes in the religious life of Negroes as they are related to the assimilation of Negroes into American society.

The growing importance of the new middle class in the Negro community is due to the continual differentiation of the population along occupational lines. Therefore, the new middle class is composed almost entirely of those persons who derive their incomes from services rendered as white-collar workers and as professional men and women. Despite the dreams of Negro leaders, fostered by the National Negro Business League at the turn of the century, that Negroes would organize big industries and large financial undertakings, Negroes have not become captains of industry nor even managers of large corporations. So-called "Negro" business continues to consist mainly of small retail stores catering to the personal needs of Negroes. There are a small number of insurance companies, small banks, and newspapers which constitute their larger business enterprises. The owners and managers of these enterprises constitute the upper layer of the middle class while the increasing number of Negroes in skilled occupations constitute its lowest stratum. For reasons which have been indicated, in the North and West about 25 percent of the Negro population is able to maintain middle-class standards while in the South only about 12 percent are in this position.

The new Negro middle class is a new phenomenon in the Negro community because it has a different economic base and a different social heritage from the relatively small middle class which had become differentiated from the masses of Negroes by the first decade of this century.[11] This older middle class was an "aristocratic" elite in a sense because its social status and preeminence were based upon white ancestry and family and its behavior was modeled after the genteel tradition of the Old South. The upper layer derived their incomes from land but the majority of the members of the elite were employed in a large variety of occupations including positions as trusted retainers in white families. The new middle class has a different occupational basis and occupation is one of the important factors in determining status.

Since the opening of the century there had been a faith among middle-class Negroes in "Negro" business as a means of solving their social as well as economic problems. This faith was somewhat as follows: as Negroes became businessmen they would accumulate capital and give employment to Negroes and once Negroes possessed wealth, white men would respect them and accord them equality. The new middle class has accepted without the critical attitude which experience should have given them, the faith in "Negro" business as a way to social and economic salvation.

Since the emergence of the new middle-class involves the rise of the more ambitious and energetic elements among the masses of Negroes to middle-class status, this new class does not possess the genteel tradition of the older middle class. This new class is largely without social roots except the traditions of the Negro folk represented in the Spirituals. But as these Negroes rise to middle-class status they reject the folk heritage and seek to slough off any reminders of their folk inheritance. However, since their rise to the middle-class status has enabled them to marry into families with the genteel tradition of the old middle class, there is often a confusion of "aristocratic" and folk values. It is for this reason that many middle-class Negroes exhibit in their manners and behavior the characteristics of both a peasant and a gentleman. Among this new class there is much confusion as to standards of behavior and beliefs. There is a constant striving to acquire money in order to engage in conspicious consumption which provides the outward signs of status and conformity to white American standards. They all possess the same goal, which is acceptance into the white community and they all profess, at least, a desire to be integrated into the white community.

Integration for the majority of middle-class Negroes means the loss of racial identity or an escape from the lowly status of Negroes and the contempt of whites. With integration they began to remove as much as possible from the names of their various organizations anything that would identify them as Negroes. This even extended to their church organizations. The Colored Methodist Episcopal Church became the "Christian" Methodist Episcopal Church. It is significant, however, that when the middle-class leaders in the African Methodist Episcopal Church attempted to take "African" out of the name and substitute the word "American," there was a revolt on the part of the masses who demanded that "African" be retained. This incident is indicative of the general attitude of the middle class towards the African background of the Negro. While there is some outward profession of pride in African independence and identification with Africa, the middle class rejects identification with Africa and wants above all to be accepted as "just Americans." It was the new middle class which was rising to importance in the 1920s that was most bitterly opposed to the Garvey Movement which had as its goal the identification of Negroes with Africa and African interests.[12] Middle-class Negroes seize upon identification with Africa only as a means of compensating for their feeling of inferiority and improving their status in the eyes of American whites.

Despite the fact that middle-class Negroes conform to the standards of whites and accept without question the values of American society, they are still rejected by the white world. They feel this rejection more keenly than lower-class Negroes who participate less in the white man's world and conform to the standards of their own separate world. Moreover, because of their position, middle-class Negroes have an ambivalent attitude towards their identification as Negroes. On the one hand, they resent the slightest aspersion upon Negroes. When placed in competition with whites they have feelings of inadequacy and when they find themselves in close association with whites they have feelings of insecurity though they may clamor for integration into the white world.[13] They are status seekers in a double sense; they strive to keep up with the expectations of their class in the Negro community and they seek or hope to gain status in the white world. In order to maintain high standards of consumption often both husband and wife work but they constantly complain of the "rat race" to maintain life as they would live it. They live frustrated lives despite their efforts to compensate for their feelings of inferiority and insecurity. They have little time for leisure and the enjoyment of what they call the "cultural" things of life. As a matter of fact, they have little appreciation of music or art and they read very little since reading has not become a tradition in the new middle class.

Their ambiguous position in American society together with their recent rise to middle-class status are reflected in the religious behavior and attitudes of middle-class Negroes. There is first a tendency for middle-class Negroes to sever their affiliation with the Baptist and Methodist churches and join the Presbyterian, Congregational, and Episcopal churches. The middle-class Negroes who continue their affiliation with the Baptist and Methodist churches choose those churches with intelligent ministers and a relatively large middle-class membership. As a consequence there is a solid core of the Negro middle class that continues to be affiliated with the Negro church. However, middle-class Negroes continue their affiliation with the Negro church for a number of reasons. Their families may have been associated with the churches and the churches which they have known since childhood provide a satisfying form of religious worship. Although many middle-class Negroes continue to be affiliated with the church, the church is no longer the center of social life for them as for the lower class. They are members of professional and business associations and Greek letter fraternal organizations, though "social" clubs constitute the vast majority of these other forms of organized social activities. Some are thus able to satisfy their striving for status outside the church. But for others it is necessary to leave the Baptist and Methodist churches and join the Presbyterian, Congregational, and Episcopal churches in order to satisfy the desire for status.

The striving for status and the searching for a means to escape from a frustrated existence is especially marked among the middle-class Negroes who cannot find a satisfactory life within the regular Negro church organization. This probably accounts for the fact that during the past two decades middle-class Negroes have been joining the Catholic church.[14] Sometimes they send their children to Catholic schools, where they will receive a discipline not provided in the public schools for Negroes. Very often after joining the Catholic church with the expectation that they will escape from their status as Negroes, they find that they are still defined as Negroes by whites. Some middle-class Negroes in their seeking to find escape from the Negro identification have gone from the Catholic church to the Christian Science church and then to the Bahaist church. Moreover, there is a tendency among middle-class Negroes to be attracted to Moral Rearmament, hoping that they would find a group in which they could lose completely their identification as Negroes and escape from their feelings of inferiority and insecurity. A small intellectual fringe among middle-class Negroes have affiliated with the Unitarian church. But some of them may still attend more or less surreptitiously the Methodist and Baptist churches on Friday nights.

This type of dual church affiliation is more characteristic of Negro professional men who affiliate with churches mainly for social and professional reasons. Some professional Negroes affiliate with a church which their friends or middle-class Negroes attend, and at the same time affiliate with churches attended by the lower class who are their clients. They are representative of the growing number of middle-class Negroes who have a purely secular outlook on the world. Some of them express contempt for religion and do not attend church though they may pretend to have some church affiliation. Since they have neither an intellectual heritage nor a social philosphy except a crude opportunism which enables them to get by in the white man's world, they may turn to all forms of superstition. This is because they are still haunted by the fears and beliefs which are a part of their folk heritage. They are often interested in "spiritual" and "psychic" phenomena. Very often the real religious feelings and faith of middle-class Negroes are expressed in their obsession with poker and other forms of gambling.[15]

The religious behavior and outlook of the middle-class Negroes is a reflection of their ambiguous position as Negroes rise to middle-class status and become increasingly integrated into the American community. To the extent that they are becoming really assimilated into American society, they are being beset by the religious dilemmas and doubts of the white middle-class Americans. On the other hand, for the masses of Negroes, the Negro church continues to be a refuge, though increasingly less of a refuge, in a hostile white world.

CONCLUSION

In this concluding chapter, we shall summarize the main points brought out in this study. The important role of religion in the social organization of American Negroes has been due to the conditions under which Negroes were introduced into the New World and to their subordination and relative social isolation in American society. No one can say what would have been the role of religion among Negroes if they had not been isolated from the main currents of American life. But under the circumstances of their subordination and isolation in American society it is difficult to imagine organized social life among Negroes without the important role of the religion and the Negro church. The Negroes were practically stripped of their social heritage and their traditional social organization was destroyed as the result of the manner in which they were enslaved and became the labor force in the plantation economy. They did not possess a historical tradition and whatever memories of their African culture were preserved through oral transmission lost their meaning when there was no longer a social organization to sustain them.

There was one element in their African heritage that was able to survive capture in Africa and the "middle passage"—dancing, the most primitive form of religious expression. The slaves were encouraged to dance during the "middle passage" and in the West Indies the slaves were forced to dance as a part of the breaking-in process. In the "shout-songs" on the Sea Islands off the coast of South Carolina and Georgia one may discover the remnants of the African religious heritage. However, no African religious cults became established on American soil. The whites did everything possible to suppress these "heathenish" practices. The Established Church with its emphasis upon a knowledge of the catechism for baptism and with its religious ritual requiring decorum did not make much progress among the slaves. It was only with the coming of the Baptist and Methodist missionaries that the slaves found a form of religion in which they could give expression to their deepest emotions. The adventitious gatherings in which tribeless men and women without even the bonds of kinship could find an ephemeral solidarity became regular meetings for religious services and a new bond of cohesion was established in the New World. Not only was a new bond with their fellow slaves established but as they joined in the religious services of their white masters their moral isolation in the white world began to break down.

So far as the slaves were permitted some autonomy in their religious life, there came into existence what might be called an "invisible institution" of the Negro church. At the same time the Negroes who were free before the Civil War left the white Methodist and Baptist church organizations in which they had a subordinate status and set up their own churches. After Emancipation the "invisible institution" of the Negro church was absorbed by the institutional churches which the Negroes who were free before the Civil War had established. There was some conflict between the two elements because the former slaves preferred a more primitive form of worship and continued the religious tradition represented in the Spirituals. Nevertheless, the two elements fused in church organizations which became the major form of organized social life among Negroes. For the masses of Negroes who were segregated from the mainstream of American life, the church communities in the South became a sort of nation within a nation.

Out of the church organizations grew other forms of organized activities among the Negroes who were free before the Civil War. After Emancipation the enlarged church organizations played an even more important role in the organization of the Negro community. They were responsible not only for economic cooperation for the purpose of erecting and buying churches, but they also provided the incentive for the pooling of the meager economic means of Negroes for mutual assistance and insurance companies. It was almost solely through the Negro church organizations that the initiative on the part of Negroes in securing an education and building educational institutions was expressed. Inasmuch as Negroes were excluded from political participation in the American community at large, the Negro church organization became the most important arena for political life among Negroes. It was in the contests carried on within these organizations that Negroes struggled for power and position and the members could exercise some choice in the selection of men to govern them. Thus, the Negro church organizations became the most effective agencies of social control among Negroes in their relatively isolated social world. And as far as the outside hostile white world was concerned, the Negro churches became a refuge or helped Negroes to become accommodated to their inferior status.

The urbanization of Negroes on a large scale, beginning with the First World War, has brought about a transformation of the Negro church and changed the outlook of Negroes upon the world and their place in the world. There has been a secularization of outlook and Negro churches have not failed to reflect this change in outlook. The regularly established Negro churches placed less emphasis upon salvation after death and directed their activities increasingly to the economic, social, and political problems of Negroes in this world. The reorganization of the religious life of Negroes in the urban environment has been influenced largely by the new class structure of Negro communities, especially in the North, which is the result of the increasing occupational differentiation of the Negro population. Among the upper strata there has been a shift from the Baptist and Methodist churches to the Presbyterian, Episcopalian, and Congregational churches. The lower strata who became lost in the impersonal atmosphere of the large city churches and longed for the intimate association of the small churches of the South where they could give free rein to their emotions, have sought a more congenial religious worship in the "storefront" churches. A more important change among the lower strata has expressed itself in the various holiness cults which seek a return to a primitive form of Christianity. The most radical deviation from the traditional religious orientation of Negroes has been in those cults which enable the Negro to escape from his racial identification and exalt secular nationalistic aims.

Since the urbanization of the Negro population has been due to broader changes in the economic and social organization of American life, it has been responsible for the increasing integration of Negroes into the mainstream of American civilization. As a result of the increasing integration, the social organization of Negro communities has been changed. And since the church has been the main form or focus of organized social life among Negroes it has been affected by integration. One of the consequences is that the church is no longer the refuge for Negroes that it was formerly. In response to the changing position of the Negro churches has been the emergence of the Gospel Singers, whose gospel songs express the deep religious feelings of the Negro masses who are increasingly exposed to life in the American community. They sing their gospel songs which are a blend of sacred and secular music, not only in Negro churches but address them to the white world as well which is beginning to sing them too.

One of the most important results of the new stratification of the Negro community has been the emergence of a relatively large new middle class, which at the same time is the most advanced element in the process of integration. Although the new middle class seeks identification with and acceptance by the white middle class, it is rejected by the latter. Moreover, the new middle class has rejected the Negro heritage, including the religious heritage. As a consequence this class occupies an ambiguous position in relation to both Negroes and whites. In its efforts to escape from its frustrations and dilemmas the new Negro middle class sometimes abandons religion altogether but more often shifts its affiliation from church to church or from one religious fad to another. Sometimes they became interested in "spiritual" and "psychic" phenomena and other forms of superstition including dependence upon "luck" and "chance." However, to the extent that they are truly assimilated in the culture of the white middle class, they experience the same religious doubts and dilemmas as whites of the same class.

The important role of religion and the Negro church in the social organization of the American Negroes has been due to the restricted participation of Negroes in American society. And as a consequence the Negro church has left its imprint upon practically every aspect of Negro life. The Negro church has provided the pattern for the organization of mutual aid societies and insurance companies. It has provided the pattern of Negro fraternal organizations and Greek letter societies. It has provided the pattern of administration and control of the Negro schools so far as they have been under the control of Negroes. Since, as we have seen, the pattern of control and organization of the Negro church has been authoritarian, with a strong man in a dominant position, the same pattern has characterized other Negro organizations. The petty tyrants in the Negro churches have their counterparts in practically all other Negro organizations. As a consequence, Negroes have had little education in democratic processes. Moreover, the Negro church and Negro religion have cast a shadow over the entire intellectual life of Negroes and have been responsible for the so-called backwardness of American Negroes. Sometimes an ignorant preacher backed by the white community has been able to intimidate Negro scholars and subvert the true aim of an educational institution. It is only as a few Negro individuals have been able to escape from the stifling domination of the church that they have been able to develop intellectually and in the field of art. This development is only being achieved on a broader scale to the extent that Negroes are being integrated into the institutions of the American community and as the social organization of the Negro community, in which the church is the dominant element, crumbles as the "walls of segregation come tumbling down."

NOTES

Chapter 1: The Religion of the Slaves

1. This statement will appear to be in sharp disagreement with the position of Melville J. Herskovits who in his *The Myth of the Negro Past* (New York, 1924) undertakes to show that African survivals can be discovered in almost all phases of Negro life in the United States. However, in arranging the areas of Negro concentration in the New World on a scale according to the intensity of African survivals, he places the area of most intense survival in Surinam and says concerning the United States that it can be set off "from the rest of the New World as a region where departure from African modes of life was greatest, and where such Africanisms as persisted were carried through in generalized form, almost never directly referable to a specific tribe or a definite area." *Ibid.,* p. 122.

2. See Bureau of the Census, *Negro in the United States, 1920–32,* p. 78.

3. See E. Franklin Frazier, *The Negro in the United States,* revised (New York, 1957), Chap. 1, concerning the manner in which the Negro was completely stripped of his African social heritage.

4. Lewis C. Gray, *History of Agriculture in the Southern United States to 1860* (New York, 1941), Vol. I, pp. 534–35.

5. "Voyages . . . de la Louisiane," Vol. III, pp. 169–70, by C. C. Robin, in Ulrich B. Phillips, ed., *Plantation and Frontier: Documents: 1649–1863* (Cleveland, 1909), p. 31.

6. See Ulrich B. Phillips, *American Negro Slavery* (New York, 1936), Chap. 11, where the author takes the position that slave trading was uneconomical and that it was generally condemned.

7. Quoted in Frederic Bancroft, *Slave-Trading in the Old South* (Baltimore, 1939), p. 365.

8. See *ibid., passim.*

9. See Lorenzo D. Turner, *Africanisms in the Gullah Dialect* (Chicago, 1949), p. 40.

10. See the author's *The Negro Family in the United States* (Chicago, 1939), Part I, concerning the Negro family during slavery.

11. W. E. B. DuBois, *Some Efforts of the American Negroes for Their Own Betterment* (Atlanta, Ga., 1898).

12. P. Mercier, "The Fon in Dahomey," in *African Worlds* (London, 1954), p. 234.

13. See Helen T. Catterall, ed., *Judicial Cases Concerning American Slavery and the Negro* (Washington, D.C., 1926), Vol. I, p. 57. See also Lorenzo J. Greene, *The Negro in Colonial New England* (New York, 1942), Chap. 10.

14. C. F. Pascoe, *Two Hundred Years of the S.P.G.: An Historical Account of the Society for the Propagation of the Gospel in Foreign Parts* (London, 1901), Vol. I, pp. 1–7.

15. See *ibid.,* p. 16, concerning some of the activities of one missionary.

16. See "The Bishop of London's Letter to the Masters and Mistresses in the English Plantations," quoted in Charles C. Jones, *The Religious Instruction of Negroes in the United States* (Savannah, 1842), p. 16.

17. See Arthur Ramos, *The Negro in Brazil* (Washington, D.C., 1939).

18. Marcus W. Jernegan, "Slavery and Conversion in the American Colonies," *The American Historial Review,* Vol. XXI (April 1916), pp. 504–27.

19. Carter G. Woodson, *The History of the Negro Church,* 2nd edn. (Washington, D.C., 1921), Chap. 2.

20. Joseph Tracy, *A History of the Great Awakening* (Boston, 1892), pp. 81–82.

21. See Catherine C. Cleveland, *The Great Revival in the West, 1797–1805* (Chicago, 1916), and Elizabeth K. Nottingham, *Methodism and the Frontier* (New York, 1941).

22. See, for example, the opinion of Herskovits, concerning the influence of African river-cults. "Social History of the Negro," in Carl Murchison, *A Handbook of Social Psychology* (Worcester, Mass., 1935), pp. 256–57.

23. See *Proceedings of the Meeting in Charleston, South Carolina, May 13–15, 1845 on the Religious Instruction of the Negroes* (Charleston, S.C., 1845).

24. See *African Worlds* with an "Introduction" by Daryll Forde (London, 1954), which contains studies of the world-outlook and religious attitudes of a number of African peoples.

25. It seems that slaves with certain tribal backgrounds were more addicted to suicide than others. Suicide was regarded by some slaves, it appears, as a means of returning to their homeland. See "Practical Rules for the Management and Medical Treatment of Negro Slaves in the Sugar Colonies," by a Professional Planter (London, 1803), in Ulrich B. Phillips, *Documentary History of American Industrial Society: Plantation and Frontier Documents: 1649–1863* (Cleveland, 1909), Vol. II, pp. 128–29.

26. See Susan M. Fickling, *Slave-Conversion in South Carolina: 1830–1860* (University of South Carolina, 1924), p. 18.

27. James G. Frazer, *Passages of the Bible* (London, 1932), pp. ix–x.

28. Rev. Thomas S. Bacon, *Sermons Addressed to Masters and Servants.* Published *in the Year 1743* (Winchester, Va., *circa* 1813), pp. 142–43.

29. See Miles M. Fisher, *Negro Slave Songs in the United States* (Ithaca, 1953), and John Lovell, "The Social Implications of the Negro Spiritual," *Journal of Negro Education* (October 1939).

30. Lydia Parrish, *Slave Songs of the Georgia Sea Islands* (New York, 1942), pp. 54–92.

31. R. R. Marett, *The Threshold of Religion* (London, 1914), p. 175.

32. It is of interest to note in passing that whereas the idea of Providence is conspicuous in the religion of the American Negro, the idea of a Fate is apparently absent. In a recent study both ideas of Providence and Fate are to be found in the religious conceptions of West African Negroes. See Meyer Fortes, *Oedipus and Job in West African Religion* (Cambridge, 1959).

33. Howard Thurman, *The Negro Spiritual Speaks of Life and Death* (New York, 1947), pp. 13–14.

34. James W. Johnson, ed., *The Book of American Negro Spirituals* (New York, 1937), pp. 123–24.

35. James W. Johnson, *The Second Book of American Negro Spirituals* (New York, 1933), pp. 93–94.

36. R. Nathaniel Dett, *Religious Folk-Songs of the Negro* (Hampton, Va., 1927), p. 124.

37. *Ibid.,* p. 126.

38. *Ibid.,* p. 123.

39. Johnson, *The Second Book of American Negro Spirituals,* p. 30.

40. Johnson, *The Book of American Negro Spirituals,* pp. 89–90.

41. Robert Anderson, *From Slavery to Affluence: Memories of Robert Anderson, Ex-Slave* (Hemingford, Nebr., 1927), pp. 22–23.

42. Frederika Bremer, *Homes in the New World,* translated by Mary Howitt (New York, 1853), Vol. I, pp. 289–90.

43. Frederick Douglass, *Life and Times of Frederick Douglass* (Chicago, 1882), p. 31.

44. William E. Hatcher, *John Jasper, the Unmatched Negro Philosopher and Preacher* (New York, 1908).

45. Cf. Fisher, *op. cit.,* p. 187.

46. Marett, *op. cit.,* p. 175. An important differentiation may be made between the ecstatic religious behavior of the crowd that "dances" and the crowd which "acts" and thus becomes a mob. See Robert E. Park and Ernest W. Burgess, *Introduction to the Science of Sociology* (Chicago, 1924), pp. 870 ff.

Chapter 2: The Institutional Church of the Free Negroes

1. James C. Ballagh, *A History of Slavery in Virginia* (Baltimore, 1902), p. 32.

2. Helen T. Catterall, ed., *Judicial Cases Concerning American Slavery and the Negro* (Washington, D.C., 1926), Vol. I, p. 55.

3. John H. Russell, *The Free Negro in Virginia: 1619–1865* (Baltimore, 1913), pp. 40–41.

4. See references in footnote 2, p. 59, in the author's *The Negro in the United States*.

5. Ulrich B. Phillips, *American Negro Slavery* (New York, 1936), p. 428.

6. See Carter G. Woodson, "The Negroes of Cincinnati Prior to the Civil War," *The Journal of Negro History*, Vol. I (January 1916), pp. 1–22.

7. Woodson, *The History of the Negro Church*, p. 27.

8. See Woodson, *The History of the Negro Church*, Chap. 3, "Pioneer Negro Preachers."

9. See *ibid.*, pp. 56–57.

10. Quoted in *ibid.*, p. 55.

11. See, for example, *"The Negro Pew" Being an Inquiry Concerning the Propriety of Distinctions in the House of God on Account of Color* (Boston, 1837).

12. Woodson, *op. cit.*, pp. 61–65.

13. *Ibid.*, pp. 73 ff.

14. Richard Allen, *The Life, Experience and Gospel Labors of Rt. Rev. Richard Allen* (Philadelphia, n.d.), p. 12. See also Charles H. Wesley, *Richard Allen, Apostle of Freedom* (Washington, D.C., 1935), pp. 15–17.

15. See Wesley, *op. cit.*, pp. 52–53.

16. Woodson, pp. 75–77.

Chapter 3: The Negro Church—A Nation Within a Nation

1. Theophilus G. Steward, *Fifty Years in the Gospel Ministry* (Philadelphia, 1915), p. 33.

2. See E. Franklin Frazier, *The Negro Family in the United States* (Chicago, 1939), Chap. 19, "Old Families and New Classes."

3. Quoted in Fisher, *Negro Slave Songs in the United States*, pp. 189–90.

4. Susan Smedes, *A Southern Planter* (Baltimore, 1887), p. 179.

5. See Frazier, *The Negro Family in the United States*, Chap. 9, "The Downfall of the Matriarchate."

6. In one case of accommodation which was unique only because of the rationalization which the Negroes used to reconcile their habitual un-regulated sex behavior with Christian morality regarding premarital sex relations, the Negroes evolved the doctrine of "clean sheets." According to this "doctrine" it was not wrong for two *Christians* to have sex relations

outside of marriage since both were "clean sheets," and could not soil each other as would be the case if one or both were unconverted or sinners.

7. L. J. Coppin, *Unwritten History* (Philadelphia, 1920), p. 127.

8. See Benjamin T. Tanner, *An Apology for African Methodism* (Baltimore, 1867), p. 123.

9. W. E. B. DuBois, *Economic Cooperation Among American Negroes* (Atlanta, 1907), p. 54.

10. *Ibid.,* p. 57.

11. W. E. B. DuBois, *The Philadelphia Negro* (Philadelphia, 1899; reprint, Schocken Books, 1967), pp. 19–20.

12. In 1790 the Brown Fellowship Society was organized among the "free brown men" of Charleston, South Carolina, to relieve widows and orphans in "the hour of their distresses, sickness and death. . . ." The membership of the Society was restricted to fifty persons who paid an admission fee of fifty dollars. See E. Horace Fitchett, "The Traditions of the Free Negroes in Charleston, South Carolina," *Journal of Negro History,* Vol. 25, pp. 139–52.

13. DuBois, *Economic Cooperation Among American Negroes,* p. 94.

14. See Arthur Raper, *Preface to Peasantry* (Chapel Hill, 1926), p. 374.

15. See Harold Van Buren Voorhis, P. M., *Negro Masonry in the United States* (New York, 1940), pp. 3–22; and Charles H. Brooks, *A History and Manual of the Grand United Order of Odd Fellows in America* (Philadelphia, 1893), pp. 19–20.

16. *Why You Should Become a Knight and Daughter of Tabor,* p. 13. Pamphlet in the Moorland Foundation, Howard University, Washington, D.C. See also Booker T. Washington, *The Story of the Negro* (New York, 1909), Vol. II, pp. 158–60.

17. W. P. Burrell and D. E. Johnson, *Twenty-five Years History of the Grand Fountain of the United Order of True Reformers* (Richmond, Va., 1909), p. 12.

18. W. J. Trent, Jr., *Development of Negro Life Insurance Enterprises,* Master's Thesis (University of Pennsylvania, 1932), p. 32.

19. Carter G. Woodson, *The Education of the Negro Prior to 1861* (New York, 1915), p. 18.

20. *Ibid.,* pp. 140–41.

21. See, for example, the resolutions passed by the African Methodist Episcopal Church in 1835 in Grace Naomi Perry, "The Educational Work of the African Methodist Episcopal Church prior to 1900," unpublished Master's Thesis (Howard University, Washington, D.C., 1948), pp. 15–21.

22. Secured during an interview.

23. Tanner, *An Apology for African Methodism,* p. 251.

24. Frazier, *The Negro in the United States,* p. 429.

25. See Woodson, *The History of the Negro Church,* p. 172.

26. See Perry, *op. cit., passim.*

27. Stephen C. Campbell, "The Influence of Negro Baptists on Secondary Education in South Carolina," unpublished Master's Thesis (Wayne University, Detroit, Mich., 1947).

28. See Woodson, *The History of the Negro Church,* Chap. 11, "The Call of Politics."

29. Henry M. Turner, *Life and Times of Henry M. Turner* (Atlanta, 1917), p. 23.

30. Woodson, *The History of the Negro Church,* pp. 236–38.

31. Samuel D. Smith, *The Negro Congress, 1870–1901* (Chapel Hill, 1940), p. 8.

32. DuBois, *The Negro Church,* p. 57.

33. The suicide rate among Negroes, it may be noted here, has always been much lower than among whites.

34. See Charles S. Johnson, *Shadow of the Plantation* (Chicago, 1934), Chap. 5, for description of Negro church services and sermons of Negro preachers in rural Black Belt County in Alabama. See also J. Mason Brewer, *The Word on the Brazos* (Austin, Tex., 1953), for Negroes' reaction to their preachers.

35. It is very likely that in the minds of the simple rural Negroes, the image of God conformed to that of a kindly white planter. The writer heard a Negro preacher in rural Alabama declare in a sermon that "Pharaoh was a nigger and like all niggers who get power he oppressed the Jews who were God's chosen people."

Chapter 4: Negro Religion in the City

1. "Letters of Negro Migrants of 1916–1918," *Journal of Negro History,* Vol. IV (1919), pp. 290–340; and "Additional Letters of Negro Migrants," *ibid.,* pp. 412–65.

2. See St. Clair Drake and Horace R. Cayton, *Black Metropolis* (New York, 1945), Part III.

3. See Benjamin E. Mays and Joseph W. Nicholson, *The Negro's Church* (New York, 1933), p. 156.

4. See *ibid.,* pp. 154 ff.

5. In an analysis of 100 sermons Mays and Nicholson found that 26 dealt with practical affairs, 54 were predominantly other worldly, and 20 were highly doctrinal. Mays and Nicholson, *op. cit.,* p. 59. Since this study was made in 1933, there is every indication that the percentage of practical sermons has increased.

6. The pastor of a large Baptist church in Philadelphia, the Reverend Marshall Sheppard, was appointed by President Franklin D. Roosevelt as Recorder of Deeds for the District of Columbia.

7. Vattel E. Daniel, "Ritual and Stratification in Chicago Negro Churches," *American Sociological Review,* Vol. 7, p. 359.

8. See Mays and Nicholson, *op. cit.,* p. 107.

9. Mays and Nicholson, *op. cit.,* p. 313.

10. Ira de A. Reid, "Let Us Prey!" *Opportunity,* Vol. 4 (September 1926), pp. 274–78.

11. *Ibid.,* p. 275.

12. See Mays and Nicholson, *op. cit.,* Chap. 16.

13. See the classification in Raymond J. Jones, *A Comparative Study of Religious Cult Behavior Among Negroes with Special Reference to Emotional Conditioning Factors,* Master's Thesis (Howard University, Washington, D.C., 1929), pp. 3–6.

14. See Drake and Cayton, *op. cit.,* pp. 641–46.

15. *Ibid.,* p. 633.

16. *Op. cit.,* p. 357–58.

17. Drake and Cayton, *op. cit.,* p. 637.

18. Quoted in *ibid.,* p. 639.

19. See Arthur Huff Fauset, *Black Gods of the Metropolis* (Philadelphia, 1944), Chap. 2.

20. *Ibid.,* p. 14.

21. *Ibid.,* p. 15.

22. See Robert A. Parker, *The Incredible Messiah* (Boston, 1937), and Fauset, *op. cit.,* Chap. 6.

23. Parker, *op. cit.,* p. 9.

24. See *ibid.,* p. 30.

25. Fauset, *op. cit.,* pp. 56 ff.

26. It appears that some Negroes have given up their meager savings when they entered the "kingdom" or "Heaven." But it is likely that Father Divine has received more substantial support from white people. The Internal Revenue Service, it seems, has never been able to discover the source of income of Father Divine who, being God, is supposed to own everything in the world.

27. Fauset, *op. cit.,* pp. 61, 66.

28. Parker, *op. cit.,* pp. 58–59.

29. Frank Rasky, "Harlem's Religious Zealots," *Tomorrow,* Vol. 9 (November, 1949), pp. 11–17.

30. *Ibid.,* p. 11.

31. *Ibid.,* p. 14.

32. Fauset, *op. cit.,* p. 26.

33. *Ibid.,* p. 26.

34. *Ibid.,* p. 26.

35. Drake and Cayton, *op. cit.,* p. 642.

36. See Fauset, *op. cit.,* Chap. 4.

37. *Ibid.,* p. 39.

38. See Fauset, *op. cit.,* Chap. 5.

39. *Ibid.,* p. 41.

40. See Fauset, *op. cit.,* p. 42.

41. See Fauset, *op. cit.,* pp. 46 ff. Fauset was able to secure only through an ex-member, and through the neglect of another member, access to the Holy Koran. He felt that he would be violating a trust to divulge all the contents of the Holy Koran. Footnote, p. 45.

Chapter 5: The Negro Church and Assimilation

1. Joshual fit de battle of Jericho,
Jericho, Jericho,
Joshua fit de battle of Jericho,
And de walls came tumbling down.

Mary White Ovington, *The Walls Came Tumbling Down* (New York, 1947; reprint, Schocken Books, 1970).

2. See Frazier, *The Negro in the United States,* Part 3, "The Negro Community and Its Institutions."

3. See the proposal of Dr. George E. Haynes of the Federal Council of Churches, quoted in Drake and Cayton, *Black Metropolis,* p. 683.

4. Cf. "Racial Assimilation in Secondary Groups," in Robert E. Park, *Race and Culture* (Glencoe, Ill., 1950), Chap. 16.

5. See Drake and Cayton, *op. cit.,* pp. 650–54, concerning the rebellion of the lower classes against the church.

6. Arna Bontemps, "Rock, Church, Rock," in Sylvester C. Watkins, ed., *Anthology of American Negro Literature* (New York, 1944), p. 431.

7. Willis Laurence James, "The Romance of the Negro Folk Cry in America," *Phylon,* Vol. XVI (1955), p. 23.

8. See *Washington Afro-American,* 5 April, 1960, for featured article on front page concerning death and funeral of Thelma Greene, at which a member of the Robert Martin Singers of Chicago sang a solo, "God Specializes," causing a number of persons to faint and to be carried out by nurses.

9. Interview with Clara Mae Ward in Winston-Salem, who claims she is only gospel singer ever to have visited the Holy Land. "Singing for Sinners," *Newsweek,* Vol. 50 (2 September, 1957), p. 86.

10. See "The Revolt of Negro Youth," *Ebony* (May 1960).

11. E. Franklin Frazier, "The Negro Middle Class and Desegregation," *Social Problems,* Vol. IV (April 1957), pp. 291–301.

12. See Frazier, *The Negro in the United States,* pp. 528–31.

13. E. Franklin Frazier, *Black Bourgeoisie* (Glencoe, Ill., 1957), pp. 216ff.

14. The recent increase during the past twenty years in the number, which remains relatively small, of lower-class Negroes in the Catholic church has been due to aid provided them during the *Depression years* and the better educational facilities, as compared with the public schools, provided them by the Catholic church.

15. See *Black Bourgeoisie,* pp. 209 ff.

THE BLACK CHURCH
SINCE FRAZIER

C. ERIC LINCOLN

Foreword

E. FRANKLIN FRAZIER was one of the titans of twentieth-century sociology. He, like Charles S. Johnson, late president of Fisk University, was a luminary of the "University of Chicago School" which attracted and influenced many other distinguished Black social scientists. I had the good fortune to "intern" with Dr. Johnson at Fisk; but Frazier, who successfully resisted the siren of college administration in favor of the scholarly life, remained for me both inspiration and model until his death in 1959. It is with humility and continuing admiration that I address the task of a complement to his work on the Black Church. Professor Frazier's death cut short an exciting sociological commentary on the Blackamerican and his times. No one else has ever said with such authority and such verve what he communicated to America in *The Negro in the United States* or *Black Bourgeoisie*. His untimely death deprived a nation of his careful analysis of what I have called the "Savage Sixties," a very critical period in the life of America. How he would have interpreted the remarkable phenomenon of Martin Luther King, Jr., and his nonviolent crusade among American Blacks, we shall never know. The Black Muslims, after having been around for decades, came to prominence only after his death. We miss his assessment of "Black power," the "third world," the drug culture, and new trends in Black religion. It falls to others like myself to carry on as best we may in his tradition without presuming to add luster to his name.

C. ERIC LINCOLN

Kumasi Hill
Antioch, Tennessee
September 1973

1

INTRODUCTION

It was roughly twenty years ago that E. Franklin Frazier first conceived his "Evolution of Religion Among American Negroes" as the Frazer Lecture in Social Anthropology at the University of Liverpool. It has been only ten years since the Frazer Lecture, augmented with new materials and refocused to treat more specifically "the role of religion in the social organization of Negro life in the United States," [1] emerged as *The Negro Church in America.* Ten years is a short time in which to measure "change" in the area of religious practices. Religion, like law, by its very nature and by the ultimate implications of its meaning for its practitioners, is not expected to register change with every shift of the wind in the ongoing life of the community. Indeed, it is the stability of religion, its tradition of endurance, its transcendence of the social flux which enables men to find in it the security and assurance they need to rescue them from the meaninglessness of change *qua* change. When the "invisible institution" [2] sang of that "Old-time Religion," its reference was to a kind of religion remembered for its faithfulness and consistency. It was a religion which had been tried and proven worthy of the testimonials of time.

Yet there is something anomalous about religion. Religion *does* change and religions *do* change. Change may be superficial before it is finally structural and systemic. But change does take place, and in religion change mirrors the social flux—which is to suggest that changing religious values may be a fairly accurate index of new perceptions men have about themselves and their relationships, as well as of new anxieties generated by change itself. "Enduring religion" endures—as it was meant to, transcending the flux and integrating the totality of experiences by which human life is gauged and evaluated. It is the *nature* of its endurance that gives religion its characteristic reliability. Religion alone has the ability to address itself effectively to what is new and evocative while retaining the assurances of what is settled and traditional —appearing at once to change with changing institutions and to persist through change unaffected by any history but its own. To understand the religious history of a people is to know quite a lot about their politics, their social habits, their hopes and aspirations, their fears, their failures, their understanding of who they are and what life holds for them. A close reading of the religious history of medieval Europe or of Colonial America is a revealing commentary on the *whole* history of these eras and the personalities who illustrated them. In societies where a common religion is acknowledged as a total way of life—as in the case of Islam, or classical Judaism, or of certain African religions—all history is read and interpreted through the perspective of religion, that of believers and nonbelievers alike.

The projection of history interpreted through the prism of religion can be a powerful device for the accentuation of group consciousness and for distinguishing those who may be "heirs to the promise" from those who are mere obstructionists to fulfillment and who, for that reason, will have to be dealt with. There is no fire, no zeal to compare to that which derives from one's personal religion rightly understood. Countless wars, pogroms, and jihads have been carried out in the interpretation of the requirements of the faith. Dissenters have been beheaded, revisionists have been burned, and unbelievers have been fed to carnivores kept handy for that purpose. And while contemporary religious commitment is usually thought of as too sophisticated (or too attenuated) to command such aggressive assiduity, among the faithful the primeval memories are never far from the surface of concern.

The tragedy of contemporary Northern Ireland is a case in point. The establishment of modern Israel and Bangladesh, although enormously complicated by international politics, economics, and military considerations, may well be counted as corroborative evidence. In the United States the Black Muslims are feared and suspected by some sections of the population, and the interdenominational evangelistic crusade known as "Key 73" has excited the concern of some segments of the American Jewish community who see its proselytizing zeal as a threat to the Jewish interest in the religious cultivation or reclamation of the religiously noncommitted within what they have traditionally considered their private cultural province.

The point is that a society or a community that is religiously alert will invariably react to whatever may be perceived as a religious innovation because whatever is new is perceived as an implied threat or contradiction to what has already been settled by history and confirmed by tradition. The "innovators" seldom see their new doctrine or practice as innovation but are quite likely to find its justification, or indeed its roots or requirements, in precisely the "Old-time Religion" to which all parties appeal as *jus canonicum*.

To retrace our steps a bit, it would be difficult to define America as "religiously alert" without some statement of qualification. Alertness can take two forms: there can be, in the case of religion, an *internal* alertness which addresses itself to the quality of the expression of the faith; and there can be an *external* alertness which functions in a groundskeeper's role with no concern other than to stave off intrusion and the violation of the premises, although the estate itself may be near ruin from internal decay. This preoccupation with territoriality has been a major bar to church union at a time when most American denominations can only point to diminishing impact and diminishing returns despite the maintenance of traditional denominational and territorial prerogatives. There seems to be no necessary relationship between territoriality and spirituality, a proposition which brings us finally to a discussion of Black religion, which is what this book is about.

The "Negro Church" that Frazier wrote about no longer

exists. It died an agonized death in the harsh turmoil which tried the faith so rigorously in the decade of the "Savage Sixties," for there it had to confront under the most trying circumstances the possibility that "Negro" and "Christian" were irreconcilable categories. The call to full manhood, to *personhood,* and the call to Christian responsibility left no room for the implications of being a "Negro" in contemporary America. With sadness and reluctance, trepidation and confidence, the Negro Church accepted death in order to be reborn. Out of the ashes of its funeral pyre there sprang the bold, strident, self-conscious phoenix that is the contemporary Black Church.

Now we have said that the characteristic principle of institutional religion is its propensity to reflect social change while remaining essentially unchanged itself. As such it permits man to "grow" without separating himself from the security and nurture that growth demands, and it reduces the risk of experimentation. So long as its anchorage is secure in the rock of the commonly recognized faith, adventurous religion may be as proliferate in its forms as disparate social needs demand. Black religion then is in essence a contemporary expression of a settled and traditional faith. The Black Church is not the "Negro Church" radicalized; rather it is a conscious departure from the critical norms which made the Negro Church what it was. The Negro Church died in the moral and ethical holocaust of the Black struggle for self-documentation because the call to Christian responsibility is in fact first and foremost a call to human dignity and therefore logically inconsistent with the limitations of Negro-ness. As man cannot serve God and mammon, neither can he be both in the image of God and not in God's image. Yet the Negro Church which died lives on in the Black Church born of its loins, flesh of its flesh, for there are no disjunctions in religion. Protestantism is not Roman Catholicism, and Islam is not Judaism. Neither are Black religion and the Black Church a mere reconstitution of the religious travail of Black people in America. The times shape the tenor of the faith. The substance of belief is its own continuity.

The Negro Church is dead because the norms and

presuppositions which structured and conditioned it are not the relevant norms and presuppositions to which contemporary Blacks who represent the future of religion in the Black community can give their asseveration and support. The Black Church is or must become the characteristic expression of institutionalized religion for contemporary Blackamericans because it is the perfect counterpart of the Black man's present self-perception and the way he sees God and man, particularly the white man, in a new structuring of relationships from which he emerges freed of the traditional proscriptions that compromised his humanity and limited his hope.

The civil rights movement of the Sixties, while politically motivated, raised fundamental issues for the Black Church and for American Christianity as well. Once the Montgomery, Alabama, campaign for civil rights and human dignity had, under the leadership of a Black clergyman, caught the imagination of Black people everywhere, the meaning and integrity of the Black Church itself became an issue. The Black Church* had been born of the travail of slavery and oppression. Its very existence was the concrete evidence of the determination of Black Christians to separate themselves from the white Christians, whose cultural style and spiritual understanding made no provision for racial inclusiveness at a level acceptable to Black people. Ever since Richard Allen and his Black fellow worshippers had been forcibly ejected from Philadelphia's St. George Methodist Church as they knelt in prayer in a segregated gallery,[3] the resulting establishment of a separate Church had symbolized even at its beginning the Blackamerican's commitment to dignity and self-determination. Yet the history and the development of the Black Church, like that of most institutions of the Black underculture, could not and did not escape the problems of ambivalence. Characteristically, as Du Bois put it, "we are of two minds," and nowhere has this double-consciousness been more apparent than in the attempt of Blackamericans to come to terms with the implications of

* Having made a distinction between the "Negro Church" and the "Black Church," I will henceforth only make reference to the "Black Church," except in those cases where an explicit comparison with the "Negro Church" is intended.

their faith and the problems of being Black in white America. The question has always been: How black is black in the context of the faith? The Black Church has always stood as the *symbol* of freedom, even when the exigencies of the times made it a "Negro" Church. But it was never completely unanimous on the issue of whether it must not also be the *instrument* of freedom—a dilemma which shadows it to this day. Perhaps it is enough that it has produced some of freedom's most celebrated leadership—Nat Turner, Henry McNeil Turner, Adam Clayton Powell, Jr., Martin Luther King, Jr., and Malcolm X, to name a handful—but the Negro Church *qua* Church traditionally courted such a conservative image as to have seldom been considered a threat to prevailing social values. The willingness to let Jesus bear the burdens of resisting an oppressive social order or to rely quite literally upon the might and protection of a God–paladin became early facets of institutionalized Black Christianity. The notions of meekness and suffering, of defense and self-indictment are still strongly rooted in the contemporary Black Church, though certainly not with the tenacity of former times when survival and submission were two sides of the same coin.

In consequence, when Martin Luther King, Jr.'s, Montgomery Improvement Association, growing out of the Black churches of Montgomery [4] raised anew the question of the definition of the Black Church's responsibility as an agent of social change. The formation of the Southern Christian Leadership Conference [5] *seemed* to define the Church's responsibility in terms of overt social action. But in practice, those Church leaders associated with SCLC seldom involved themselves beyond the matter of financial support for the movement. The involvement of its minister, in most cases, provided a sufficient vicarious participation to satisfy the congregation. Hence the Church was involved and *not* involved. The security intentions of such a strategy, and the futility of such intentions, were soon to be illustrated by the savage bombing of Black churches all over the South. The mere fact that a church permitted a protest meeting to be held anywhere on its premises became sufficient cause for that church to be bombed and burned to the ground by "persons unknown." In Birmingham, Alabama, four little girls were murdered when some "person unknown" threw a bomb from a speeding car into the Sixteenth Street Baptist Church. Scores of others gathered there for Sunday morning worship were injured. The Sixteenth Street Church had become an important rallying ground for Black protest in Birmingham, and now the message to the Black Church was made clear, written in the blood of Black children: it was not enough that the Church as a congregation disassociate itself from the freedom movement, the Church buildings themselves must be closed to the community, or the buildings *and* the people would be bombed out of existence. The message was clear, but it was not effective—except possibly as a catalyst to urge a review of the traditional posture of the Negro Church. Some groups like the Deacons for Defense in Louisiana armed themselves and vowed to protect their churches with their lives, if necessary. But the more dramatic defiance was that of the Black clergy. In some cases pastors lost their pulpits because of their commitment to the "cause." The institutionalized Church was not yet prepared to give up its conventional insularity from the realities which conditioned its existence, nor for that matter, were *all* Black clergymen; but the tide of thinking had turned. The rationale for quietism had been vitiated. The Black Church was suddenly in a mood to hear, if not yet to follow, the urgings of a new leadership militantly committed to new and sometimes disturbing expectations of itself, the Black Church, God, and society. It did not expect much from traditional American "white" Christianity, and as Black religion gained self-confidence, it would expect even less.

Amid the crunching of nightsticks, the snarling of dogs, the screaming of epithets, the barring of Black Christians from white churches, and the escalating murder of Blacks who protested it all, the white Church as a point of spiritual reference lost its luster, and the Negro Church, which had accommodated itself to the notion of a superior morality (however obscure) in the white man's expression of their common faith, now thoroughly disillusioned, consigned itself to its own history. The Black Church as a self-conscious, self-assertive, inner-directed institution was born, but as the Black Church is not the Negro Church reborn, neither is it the white Church replicated. And yet in some sense it is both of these. Ironically, the white Church in America is the principal *raison d'être* for the Black Church, for just as the white Church permitted and tolerated the Negro Church, it made the Black Church necessary for a new generation of Black people who refuse to be "Negroes" and who are not impressed by whatever it means to be white.

2

THE POWER IN
THE BLACK CHURCH

FOR worldwide Christendom the decade of the Sixties will possibly be remembered as a period of great promise for "church union," the healing of the fragmented body of Christ through the coming together of the historically distinct denominations and sects. Some churches did merge. Notable among the white American denominations were the Congregationalists and the Evangelical Reformed Church,[1] the Methodists and the United Brethren,[2] and certain Presbyterian groups long separated over issues no longer seen as pertinent to the life of the Church. Other Church bodies in Canada, Africa, and Asia effected similar unions, and the daring hope of those most committed to union was that in time a United Protestant Church, having healed itself of its own spiritual and theological schizophrenia, could at last turn toward Rome. And Rome seemed in a mood that could be taken as conciliatory. The Catholics were listening, waiting, observing, and occasionally consulting—albeit "unofficially." Catholic theologians were given prominent appointments at leading Protestant seminaries, and serious, exploratory ecumenical dialogue became the order of the day wherever serious Christian leadership came together. When a leading Jesuit seminary [3] announced its desire to relocate, two leading Protestant seminaries [4] were so competitive in their invitations to the Catholic institution, as to delay an actual decision for several months. One interesting result of this newer rapprochement between Protestants and Catholics was its probable contribution to the extraordinary phenomenon of John F. Kennedy, an Irish Catholic, being elected thirty-fifth President of the United States. Never before had the Protestant Establishment allowed its liberalism to be quite so unrestrained.

By the end of the Sixties, nine Protestant denominations [5] had joined the Committee on Church Union (COCU), but the drive toward church union foundered badly in the early Seventies as more and more Protestants, fearing the loss of their traditional independence (and perhaps of their identity as well), found denominational merger less and less attractive. In the first place, all of the mergers that did in fact occur brought together "logical" groups already in the same theological or historical tradition. There were no mergers that brought into a single communion groups holding widely disparate confessional positions. After the more obvious mergers were effected, suddenly it seemed that a "united front against Communism" was somehow less compelling than before, and perhaps the restoration of the broken body of Christ might not necessarily require "a slavish uniformity" in belief and practice among all true believers. Individuals have differing tastes and requirements, even in religion. The Presbyterian groups, now united with each other as the Presbyterian Church USA, withdrew from COCU in 1973.[6]

The hope for meaningful church union in the United States was, of course, already undercut by racism long before the general disenchantment with the movement had set in. Although three Black Methodist denominations [7] were eventually committed to union after some elaborate concessions to protect them from discrimination had been offered by the white constituents, none of the three Black Baptist conventions [8] ever affiliated. None of the Black communions would ever be very likely to be comfortable with any plans that would exchange their autonomy for white control and direction. Black Christians have had a bitter experience with religion in the white man's Church, and that experience transcended slavery and freedom alike. Wherever white Christians and Black Christians had come in contact with each other in America, Black Christians had been demeaned by the white man's presumption of racial superiority. In their own churches in their own denominational structures, Black Christians had become accustomed to a sense of dignity and self-fulfillment impossible to even contemplate in the white Church in America. The Black Church created its own literature, established its own publishing houses, elected its own bishops and other administrators, founded its own colleges and seminaries, and developed its own unique style of worship. Because Black individuals themselves have frequently been unsure of their identity, and because the Black Church is itself a creature of the countercurrents of American racial proclivities, the Black Church has not always been without ambivalence in its understanding of what it is and why. At times it has seen itself as a less perfect counterpart of the white Church, striving for parity in perfection. This self-demeaning undervaluation made some "Negro" churches more "white" in their ritual behavior and their social attitudes than many of the white churches they sought to emulate. Black ministers with "Scottish-Presbyterian" accents, the distribution of church offices on the basis of skin color, the effort to exclude from the worship services every vestige of "Negro music" or "Negro emotionalism" have at times illustrated the uncertainty the Black Church has had about its role and its function.

On the other hand, the Black Church has been much maligned for being *Black*—a "nigger institution." Its deficiencies and shortcomings have been magnified, with little effort on the part of its critics to see beyond the politics, maladministration, and general insufficiencies by which it has been characterized. The implications have always been that whatever the shortcomings of the Black Church, they could somehow be removed or ameliorated by getting rid of the stigma of blackness. If Black Christians could only be somebody other than themselves, what fine people they would be. Their churches would look better, their ministers would be better educated, their programs would be more efficiently administered, and, of course, people would respect them more!

To be or not to be is not always the question. The Black

Church decided two centuries ago that it *had* to be. Now it has been pushed by fate and circumstance into deciding *what* to be and *how*.

One of the leading architects of the developing Black Church was Martin Luther King, Jr. King's contributions to the moral and political experience of America are enormous, and they transcend his more incidental relationships. Yet in the context of American tradition, King's relationship with the Black Church could scarcely have been incidental. Although fame and recognition eventually took him to the four corners of the world and gained him admission to places and presences inaccessible to lesser men of whatever color, when he first left Boston University to offer himself to God and man, despite his excellent education and preparation for the ministry, despite his eloquence, high moral character, and his promise, no doors opened to him except *Black* doors. He belonged to the Black Church whether he would or not, and when the Dexter Avenue Baptist Church of Montgomery summoned him, Dexter was symbolically and prophetically the Black Church summoning her own. Even a decade later, when Martin Luther King had won the world's acclaim, including the Nobel Peace Prize, and even as various movements were hailing him a *héro sans couleur,* a leader for all the people and every cause, so far as American Christendom was concerned his blackness was not transcended. From Riverside Church in New York City to St. Paul's in London, he spoke from the pulpits of many famous churches, but he knew and those who heard him knew that when the last amen was said, his brief mission had been concluded. One of King's biographers writes that among the dozens of offers he received following his successful leadership of the Montgomery boycott was "the pastorship of a large Northern white church."[9] There is no indication that King ever took such an invitation seriously, for when he left the Dexter Street Church in Montgomery, it was to return to Ebenezer Baptist in Atlanta, the Black church in which he was raised and nurtured. He belonged to the Black Church, and in it and for it he lived and died.

It was Martin Luther King who made the contemporary Black Church aware of its power to effect change. King was not the first Black clergyman to be a leader of social action. The history of the Black experience is replete with the names of such preacher–activists—from Nat Turner to Adam Clayton Powell, Jr. But King, first as leader of the Montgomery Improvement Association and later as founder and leader of the Southern Christian Leadership Conference, was first to put together a sustained coalition of Christian leadership at the pulpit level. In Montgomery, as King himself put it, his task was to "be militant enough to keep my people aroused to positive action and yet moderate enough to keep this fervor within controllable and Christian bounds." [10] His method was a strategy of Christian love:

> Love your enemies. . . . Let no man pull you so low as to make you hate him. . . . If you will protest courageously, and yet with dignity and Christian love, when the history books are written in future generations, the historians will have to pause to say "there lived a great people—a black people—who injected new meaning and dignity into the veins of civilization." This is our challenge and our overwhelming responsibility. [11]

While it must be left to history to determine how much dignity American civilization was able to retain after several years of Martin Luther King's rather revolutionary application of Christian love, the Black Church took on the dignity of leadership and the posture of martyrdom, which is the traditional penalty for serious leadership in civil rights. In Montgomery, the Black Church sought to convince a Christian society long committed to white supremacy and Black subjugation that love and patience and sacrifice could effect a degree of social change, even in situations encrusted with prejudice and sanctified by tradition. Of far greater significance, the Black Church had convinced itself before the decade was over that it had *power,* a potency it never even suspected.

To understand the power of the Black Church it must first be understood that there is no disjunction between the Black Church and the Black community. The Church is the spiritual face of the Black community, and whether one is a "church member" or not is beside the point in any assessment of the importance and meaning of the Black Church. Because of the peculiar nature of the Black experience and the centrality of

institutionalized religion in the development of that experience, the time was when the personal dignity of the
Black individual was communicated almost entirely through
his church affiliation. To be able to say that "I belong to Mt.
Nebo Baptist" or "We go to Mason's Chapel Methodist" was
the accepted way of establishing identity and status when there
were few other criteria by means of which a sense of self or a
communication of place could be projected. While this has
been modified to some degree in recent times as education,
vocational diversification, and new opportunities for non-
religious associations have increased, the social identity of the
Blackamerican as well as his self-perception are still to an
important degree refracted through the prism of his religious
identity. His pastor, his church, his office in the church, or
merely his denomination are important indices of who *he* is.
The Black Church, then, is in some sense a "universal church,"
claiming and representing all Blacks out of a long tradition
that looks back to the time when there was only the Black
Church to bear witness to "who" or "what" a man was as he
stood at the bar of his community. The Church still accepts a
broad-gauge responsibility for the Black community inside
and outside its formal communion. No one can die "outside the
Black Church" if he is Black. No matter how notorious one's
life on earth, the Church claims its own at death—and with
appropriate ceremony. The most colorful and protracted
funerals in the Black community are often those of
"nonchurch" figures who, by the standards of some other
communions, might be questionable candidates for the unre-
stricted attention of the Church.

Because "the Church" is still in an important sense "the
people," and because the Church leaders are still the people's
representatives, the stature of the Black Church was im-
measurably enhanced by the Montgomery affair. Not only did
the Church (and the people) win a very critical and dangerous
contest with the white Establishment of the capital city of the
old Southern Confederacy, it won the larger battle, and by its
own example, destroyed the appalling, enervating psychology
that had convinced generations of Blacks of the invincibility of
the white man and the incapacity of Black people to follow
Black leadership, or to hang together under the stress of white

disapproval. The lesson of Montgomery was possibly Dr. King's most fundamental contribution to Blackamerica, for the great boycott that lasted from December of 1955 to December of 1956 helped countless millions of Blacks all over the country to find themselves and to understand more clearly the basic anatomy of white–Black relations. What they discovered at Montgomery was a formidable panoply of myth and taboo supported by the frequent abuse of raw power that kept Black people intimidated and afraid. The Montgomery experience taught them to discount the myth, ignore the taboo, and deal with white power for what it was.

It was inevitable that the lessons of Montgomery would be tested again and that out of each new encounter there would be produced a proliferated body of experiences to be drawn upon for the refinement of strategy as the Black Church enlarged its commitment to the redignifying of its people, and to the certifying of its own relevance. The first child of the Montgomery experience was SCLC, the Southern Christian Leadership Conference. SCLC was founded in 1957 at a meeting of some sixty churchmen, most of them ministers, at Ebenezer Baptist—the church pastored by King's father in Atlanta. King was elected president, and SCLC remained his primary base of operations until his death. King's commitment to nonviolence became the operating philosophy of SCLC. Addressing itself to America's harassed and segregated Blacks, SCLC called upon them to:

> assert their human dignity [by refusing] further cooperation with evil. But far beyond this . . . we call upon them to accept Christian love in full knowledge of its power to defy evil. We call upon them to accept Christian love in full knowledge of its power to defy evil. We call upon them to understand that non-violence is not a symbol of weakness or cowardice, but as Jesus demonstrated, non-violent resistance transforms weakness into strength and breeds courage in the face of danger.[12]

The nonviolent resistance movement was both instructive and embarrassing to the white American religious Establishment. It was the perfect example of fundamental Christian ethics being put into practice. But the practitioners were Black, and their strategy of returning love for evil and nonviolent response in the face of indescribable violence was directed essentially at *white* Christians. The unjust laws the Blacks were refusing to cooperate with were laws legislated and maintained by a white Establishment proud to conceive of itself as "one nation under God, with liberty and justice for all."

A few white clergymen spoke in support of the programs of King and SCLC and promptly lost their pulpits. Others who "introduced tension" in their churches by attempting to approach the matter from a "teaching perspective" found themselves "too far ahead of the people" and desisted from their efforts. Scores of other white clergymen and some prominent white laymen supported the Black thrust for freedom and dignity by raising money and by joining the civil-disobedience demonstrations which were to rock the South for a decade after Montgomery. "Black and white together" was institutionalized in the theme song of the civil rights movement, which began with an extraordinary expression of faith: "We shall overcome . . . someday." While many of the white churchmen were undoubtedly acting out their sense of guilt, and others recognized an opportunity for national publicity and some public acclaim for taking the Gospel of Jesus Christ onto the firing line of civil rights for Black people, there were individual cases of extreme sacrifice and extraordinary heroism. Some whites (and many Blacks) lost their lives.

Montgomery and SCLC showed the Black Church its potential for power, and it was inevitable that in probing the possibilities for making that potential real, a variety of strategies would emerge, and there would be differences on which programs and policies should be given priority and which ones should be muted or abandoned. First there was a problem of jurisdiction. The National Association for the Advancement of Colored People (NAACP) and the Urban League were long established as primary institutions in the arena of civil rights. King himself had been careful not to appear in competition with the leadership of these groups, and SCLC became "Southern," or regionalized, precisely to avoid conflict with the interests of the NAACP and to supplement its work.[13] It must not appear that Black leadership was competing with itself or that there was confusion or discord in its ranks. Ironically it was within the institutional Black Church that confusion and discord first developed and, perhaps prophetically, within the huge Baptist denomination (to which King himself belonged), where the traditions of autonomy and individualism were precisely the features that were to give the Black Baptist clergy an unmatched prominence in the Freedom Movement of the Fifties and Sixties.

In 1962 a faction of more liberal members withdrew from the National Baptist Convention to form the Progressive Baptist Alliance. Dr. King figured prominently in the chain of events which eventuated in the formation of the new denomination, and in doing so, he earned the public enmity of Dr. Joseph H. Jackson, long the president and spiritual leader of the National Baptist Convention, the largest Black denomination in Protestantism. Jackson considered King an upstart, a provocateur, and ultimately a menace to the best interests of Black people and the clerical profession. "For Jackson, the role of the preacher was to bring the good news of the gospel to his flock, to save the members of his flock for Jesus, and to effect change by exemplary conduct." [14] Dr. Jackson's views were shared by many Blacks of his generation, but despite his power and personal prestige, his was not the prevailing image of the proper Black Baptist clergyman that emerged from the crises of the King era. Men like Wyatt Walker,[15] Fred Shuttlesworth,[16] Ralph Abernathy,[17] and Leon H. Sullivan [18] brought to the Baptists and to the Black Church in general a new kind of leadership that hurried along the demise of passivity in the Black Church.

Dr. Leon Sullivan's contributions, while emanating from less dramatic kinds of confrontations than those of Dr. King's SCLC, were in effect hardly less dramatic and certainly no less valuable to a people seeking power through the Church. Sullivan's own words suggest the psychological obstacles he (and all Black clerical leaders) was faced with, but they also illustrate the power potential inherent in the Black Church:

> Although [the black preacher] has been criticized . . . for what has been called lack of leadership in the colored community, the fact is that without the influence he has exerted through his church, we black people

would never have come as far as we have. . . . Every movement of significant proportions to survive in the black community has had its roots in
the colored church. . . .[19]

Sullivan, who had been an active supporter of Martin
Luther King in his various campaigns to integrate lunch
counters in the South, awoke one day to the dismal realization
that, while the lunch counters of his own city of Philadelphia
were not generally segregated in front, all the people who worked
behind those counters were white. What Black people needed
more than anything else was jobs. The dignity of an "integrated hamburger" without an integrated quarter to pay for
it seemed a specious dignity indeed. At Sullivan's initiative
four hundred Black ministers of Philadelphia launched a
"selective patronage" campaign against certain of the worst
offenders among the industries that depended heavily on Black
patronage but refused to employ Black workers. Their objective was to end job discrimination against Blacks by activating
the latent power of the Black Church and bringing it to bear
against the concerted power of big business. Despite its loca-
tion outside the South, where rigid patterns of job discrimination were "normal," the City of Brotherly Love had a dismal
record of Black employment:

Up to 1958 in Philadelphia, although the black population comprised
one-fourth of the city's population, less than one percent of the sensitive,
clerical, and "public-contact" jobs were held by black people. The jobs
blacks held fell mostly into the "service" field and into the most menial
categories. As of 1958, in all the banks in the City of Philadelphia there
were only a few colored tellers. There were absolutely no black salesman–drivers of trucks for such major soft-drink companies as Pepsi-Cola,
Coca-Cola and 7-Up. There were no full-time colored salesman–drivers of
major baking companies, or of any of the ice-cream companies . . . [or] of
oil trucks. . . . There were few black clerks in supermarkets, few colored
sales girls in department stores, and few black clerical and stenographic
workers in the large offices downtown. Everywhere you went where the
jobs were good, you saw whites, and everywhere you went where the jobs
were poor you saw blacks. And even those "black jobs" had white
bosses. . . .[20]

The "Philadelphia Four Hundred," in this case a deter-mined alliance of Black ministers, brought an end to the more blatant forms of job discrimination by the simple expedient of suggesting to their congregations that they avoid promoting the evils of discrimination by not doing business with com-panies who practiced it. Segregation in the church itself left the Black preacher uniquely situated to lead such a campaign and to follow his own suggestions, because none of the managers of the offending businesses was likely to be a member of his church, or on his board of trustees, or even an acquaintance. When a company had been visited by a Committee of Ministers and invited to hire and/or upgrade Black workers and still refused to do so, on the following Sunday each of the four hundred Black ministers "invoked Selective Patronage against the par-ticular company, declaring, we cannot in good moral con-science remain silent while members of our congregations pa-tronize companies that discriminate against the employment of our people." For three years the Black Church was locked in a silent revolution. Once the silence had been broken by a feature story in *The New York Times*,[21] so effective was the Philadelphia movement, that the "selective patronage" tech-nique soon spread to Atlanta, Detroit, New York, and other cities. But the ministers in Philadelphia went a critical step further: soon realizing that few Blacks were prepared for jobs seldom available to them, the Black Church through its Op-portunities Industrialization Centers—the first one housed in an abandoned jail—went on to provide Black people with the skills and training needed to fill the jobs selective patronage could open.[22]

Leon Sullivan, who rose from poverty in the back alleys of Charleston, West Virginia, and whose pastoral apprenticeship was served in Adam Clayton Powell's Abyssinian Baptist Church in Harlem, attributes the success of the Philadelphia Movement to prayer, moral initiative, black unity, and the fostering of an appreciation of money as a prime determinant in human behavior.[23] Prayer and moral circumspection are, of course, institutionalized in the Black Church. Indeed, its harshest critics have long accused it of consigning to prayer too much that demands immediate human attention, and of being more concerned about morality than survival. Such critics, however, are seldom sophisticated about what religion is, and in the terror and frustration of day-to-day existence in a society in which the oppressor is identified as Christian, their patience with what seems to be too great a reliance upon values and institutions that appear suspect is soon exhausted. Nevertheless, both Leon Sullivan and Martin Luther King and their movements represent *de facto social* accomplishments of the Black Church at work. As for prayer and morality they are, of course, constituent elements of any mature religion.

There is probably more unity in the Black Church than is commonly recognized. Ninety percent, possibly more, of all Blacks in America belong to five major communions in *two* denominations,[24] an impressive record when compared statistically with the distribution of members in the white Church in America. It is useful to make the point of denominational unity here, but obviously Dr. Sullivan meant unity of purpose *across* denominational lines—the kind of myth-shattering unity the Black Church had already displayed at Montgomery under the leadership of Martin Luther King. Sullivan and his associates proved again that the power inherent in the Black Church is limited only by the failure of sophisticated leadership to understand and appreciate what kind of an entity the Black Church is and to develop techniques of leadership compatible with the Church's understanding of itself and its function. The Black Church's traditional reluctance to place itself in opposition to the white power structure grew partly out of lessons learned from actual experience and partly from the vicarious understandings communicated through the projections of actual experience. The fundamental beliefs contributing to this reluctance were (1) the absolute invulnerability of the white man, and (2) the absolute vulnerability of all Black people and all Black institutions. These two convictions, formidable in themselves, were usually buttressed by (3) feelings of contingency and dependence—the recognition that, ultimately, life itself depended upon the white man's goodwill, his charitableness, or at the very least his passivity. This was the ultimate psychological conditioning at which the ideology of slavery was directed—to inoculate the slave with the notion, nay, the *certainty,* that his welfare, his status, his *life* always lay in the hands of his master. Hence the surest security was to behave in such a way as to evoke the master's active goodwill, and the greatest jeopardy was to rouse the master's annoyance or displeasure. Deliberate invisibility was sought whenever possible, because while doing nothing to attract the master's attention one way or another was risky, but certainly less hazardous than open defiance.

A fourth conviction had to do with the unreliability of Black leadership. Since all Blacks were equal in their inequality, i.e., their social distance from whites, to trust any Black leader was to assume the miraculous. Self-hatred left little room for imagining any Black man able to deliver in any contest with the white man. Black leaders were not as well prepared. They had little or no experience. Worst of all, since all Blacks were deprived, Black leaders could not resist the pressures to "sell out" for a little money or a long title. Present in this attitude was the latent assumption that Black leadership was a game which Blacks could never expect to win against whites. Hence the real goal of the Black leaders was a pay-off that would in effect permit them to win against Blacks. It was viewed as an in-group exercise in futility, well calculated to produce personal reward for the leaders but only frustration or at best some measure of catharsis for all others. At worst, a foolish or unscrupulous Black leader could bring down the wrath of the white Establishment with great suffering and increased inconvenience for those he presumed to lead.

Finally, (5) there was a moral aspect to the matter which had proved very troublesome in the past and which in various forms and guises still haunts the Black Church. Essentially it was the question of "unfaithfulness" to white supporters who in times past were relied upon for such favors as they chose to deliver—charity, philanthropic intercession, advice and counsel, commiseration, etc. Tradition has it that Black people never forget a favor and never remember a wrong. That is why, it has been argued, Black slavery was so successful and why it lasted so long. Whatever the merits of this proposition, the concern for the sensibilities of "white friends" has undoubtedly been important in the structuring of strategy and the selection (or rejection) of leadership in the Black community. Similarly the Church had to deal with the issue of the degree of the white man's culpability. The Black Muslims solved that problem

summarily by declaring the white man totally demoniac, totally depraved—a creation of Yakub, the very Prince of
Demons. Accordingly the Muslims placed the white adver-
sary outside the pale of redemption, a religious strategy calculated to reduce Black–white relations to a very elemental
level and to simplify whatever questions there might arise as to
the Muslims' proper concern for white people. But the
Muslims are not representative of normative Black religion.
The traditional Black Church was both cautioned and conditioned by its history. It could scarcely be comfortable with a
declaration that the very people who brought it the Gospel in
the first place were a race of demons beyond the scope of God's
redemption and excluded from the area of their proper Christian concern.

Like all the other elements of the syndrome we are discuss-
ing, either these attitudes now are in sharp abatement or the
problems that generate them have been redefined in a way that
permits them to be dealt with in the context of Black theology.
Yet their significance for understanding the metamorphosis of
the Black Church must not be overlooked. In summary it can
be said that the Black Church has often chosen to struggle with
the problem of whether to struggle at all with the powers and
principalities of this world, and whether such a struggle might
not question the righteousness and the sufficiency of God, who
in His own way and in His own good time sets all things right.
The notion of white invincibility and Black vulnerability and
contingency, the suspicion of Black leadership, the concern for
the white man's soul and for the divine prerogative to initiate
change—all add up to a basic, inherent conservatism. But it
also adds up to a mature religious posture that distinguishes
the Church from a mere instrument of civil rights or social
change. This is a distinction oppressed, impatient Blacks find
difficult to understand, if not at times even to perceive. And it
is a distinction which critical whites frequently refuse to ac-
knowledge when the Black Church does become aroused or
involved. But Black religion and the church which is its cultus
do have moral and ethical concerns beyond civil rights; and
they do (as indeed they must) confront issues at times on levels
at which theological considerations, psychological conditioning, and myth come into play. The leaders who have been most

successful in "gathering" the tremendous power of the Black Church are those who have been wise enough to work with the people through, and not oblivious of, the requirements of their faith. Such leadership is common in the case of individual churches or cults and is often attributed to the "charismatic attractiveness" of a particular minister or cult leader. But "charisma" is a difficult word to define, and certainly it has been stretched to cover a multitude of aptitudes not necessarily related to "spiritual gifts." In the contemporary understanding of the word, a saint and a charlatan may both be "charismatic" leaders, the only difference being what they intend to do with the money. Charismatic leaders come and go, seldom leaving any permanent imprint upon the social fabric into which their lives were woven. The Black churches have had more than their share of such, but effective leadership of the Black Church requires something more.

Although the Black Church has been the sole nexus of real power, gathered or ungathered in the Black community throughout its history, *Black Power* as a specter to plague the conscience of white America began as a slogan created by the young Black militants of the Student Non-Violent Coordinating Committee (SNCC, or "Snick"), then led by Stokley Carmichael.[25] It was the summer of 1966. The mood of the Black revolution had turned ominous. The ghetto rebellions and the accompanying destruction of white-owned property in the ghetto, the receding white liberal support for civil rights, the uncompromising stand for freedom being adopted by proliferating young-militant action groups, the discovery that the white man is *vulnerable,* that he could be hurt, and the hardening of resistance to Black demands had all contributed to racial tension that was approaching the point of explosion. Suddenly, an anguished, defiant cry for "Black Power!" pierced the pall of tension hanging over the Mississippi Delta, bounced off the cotton-choked landings at Memphis, and issued in a clamorous reverberation in Wall Street, Main Street, and Pennsylvania Avenue. It was a cry America was prepared neither to hear nor to entertain. Massachusetts' Black senator Edward Brooke complained, "That slogan has struck fear in the heart of black America as well as in the heart of white America. . . .The Negro has to gain allies—not adversaries." [26] President Lyndon B. Johnson declared, "We're not interested in black power and we're not interested in white power, but we are interested in democratic power with a small d." [27] And Martin Luther King explained: "It is absolutely necessary for the Negro to gain power, but the term Black Power is unfortunate because it tends to give the impression of black nationalism . . . " [28] and on another occasion, "For five long hours I pleaded with a group to abandon the Black Power slogan." [29]

The Black Power cry (accompanied by a raised, clenched fist) originated in the SNCC faction of a coalition of civil rights groups marching through Mississippi in a show of solidarity in the continuing struggle for racial justice. But solidarity was fast fading, and the cry for Black Power hastened its demise. Dr. Nathan Wright observes:

> People who heard the cry when it was first raised reported feelings of both understanding and apprehension. Clearly the powerless black people . . . throughout the land needed power. Yet this was a new cry. It represented a new stance, which under the potentially explosive conditions of parts of the rural South and our urban slums, could herald a threatening imbalance in the power relationships through which progress had been previously charted.
>
> The continuation of the cry quickly made clear that the fears were justified, at least in part. Old mechanisms for the purpose of work for racial justice were being challenged and judged ineffective. Under the banner of Black Power, and in the manifest breakdown of patience, long-trusted and acknowledged Negro leaders were being by-passed, if not disclaimed. . . . There was a breach in the tried and time-worn mechanisms for communication.[30]

And Wright's analysis is echoed by Gayraud Wilmore:

> The reaction within the middle class, interracial coalition that was the civil rights movement was predictable. Dismay over the turn toward black nationalism spread a blanket of gloom over liberal whites in the National Council of Churches. . . . Black church leaders such as Dr. J. H. Jackson, President of the National Baptist Convention, . . . deplored the nationalist trend. . . . Individual pastors who all along had stayed aloof from SCLC . . . were more than ever convinced that there were radical, anti-Christian elements with whom the Black church was incompatible,

working within the freedom movement. . . . The Black Christian
radicalism which had made Martin Luther King, Jr., the high priest of
the religion of civil rights . . . was giving way to a somewhat less sanctified,
less precise and less American ideology of Black Power.[31]

It is ironic that the Black Church, which had always been
the repository of Black Power, should be alarmed by the
demand for it. But it is not inexplicable. The Church wanted
power on terms it conceived to be consistent with its posture of
faith and moral responsibility. The cry of the militants was
Black Power—*by any means possible!* The Church wanted to share
the white man's power in order to fulfill its own responsibilities
to God and man. The new cry was for power because it was
politically and economically right and necessary, and because
not to have it left the white man in total control and signified
the Black man's continuing acceptance of that archaic arrangement. For a moment the Church faltered. King, who more
than any other single individual had led the Church in the
realization of its power potential, was caught off guard. He
needed time to reassess his situation in the light of an
increasingly somber mood pervading the civil rights movement
because of a number of new elements.

Some white liberals had quietly left the movement. Others
were being asked by some constituent organizations like SNCC
and CORE [32] to give up their leadership roles in order that
Blacks could have a more prominent hand in making their own
decisions. The war in Vietnam had become a major competitor
for the interest of white activists and for the conscience of the
American people. And most disturbing of all, new groups of
militant young Blacks for whom "nonviolence" was a synonym
for Tomism were springing up all over the country and gaining
prominence in the press and in the streets. Some of them were
left-wing or Marxist oriented; some were not. But a common
thread of Black nationalism, rejection of integration as a
solution to America's racial problems, and impatience with
nonviolence and "Christian love" as techniques for social
change ran through them all. To an alarming number of Black
youths the NAACP, the Urban League, and SCLC were all
organizations seen as ultimately under the control of the
enemy—the white man. New "third world" alliances were be-

ing talked about, as were new kinds of "revolutionary activity" that did not rule out "guerrilla activity" and other forms of violence.

The Black Muslims offered America's restive Black youth a cryptic promise to "treat the white man the way he *should be* treated," and Malcolm X, their fiery polemicist, dominated "Black" news on television and in the press with the teachings of the Honorable Elijah Muhammad. Muhammad's doctrine twitted "the so-called Negroes" about trying to love the white man, who "by nature, cannot love you." He offered them instead the *lex talionis*, an eye for an eye. . . .[33]

After its brief moment of dismay, almost as if with conscious determination not to relinquish its leadership initiative or lose the momentum it had generated over the preceding decade, the Black Church moved to deal with the issue of Black Power. Under the leadership of Dr. Benjamin Payton [34] the National Council of Black Churchmen was organized in New York City. NCBC was in some sense the Northern counterpart of SCLC, and its membership, particularly its leadership, tended to reflect a concentration of Black Christians in "white" denominations—i.e., Presbyterians, Episcopalians, Congregationalists, and others outside the traditional Black communions. This was to prove a serious handicap in the work and development of the organization as it sought to increase its relevance as an arm of the Black Church. As the Black Church became more self-conscious about its blackness, its wariness toward those brethren with white denominational affiliations, particularly those holding important positions in the institutional structures of the white church, would hardly be diminished by the formation of a New York-based organization. Indeed, the Black Church had never given SCLC its "official" recognition. Nevertheless, NCBC became a significant, *de facto* expression of the Black Church and a timely spokesman for its interests. Initially, it was organized to:

> discuss the almost hysterical reaction of the white clergy to Black Power, the way in which the slogan was being distorted by white churchmen and bandied about wildly and thoughtlessly by Black spokesmen, and the obvious inability of the Southern Christian Leadership Conference to

respond positively to the new situation and mobilize increasing numbers of radical Black clergy in the North for leadership in the next stage of the struggle.[35]

The first public act of NCBC was to publish in *The New York Times* [36] a statement entitled "Black Power." Its goal seems to have been to put the issue into proper perspective —theologically, historically, and practically. The statement was addressed to "four groups of people in areas where clarification . . . is of the most urgent necessity": (1) To the Leaders of America (Power and Freedom); (2) To White Churchmen (Power and Love); (3) To Negro Citizens (Power and Justice); and (4) To the Mass Media (Power and Truth). The preamble of this extraordinary statement set the tone for the message to follow by labeling the white outcry over Black Power a "variety of rhetoric [which] is not anything new but the same old problem of power and race . . ." which has existed as long as the two races have been in America. "The power of white men and the conscience of black men have both been corrupted," the statement continues. The one because "it meets little meaningful resistance from Negroes to temper it and to keep white men from aping God." The other because Black men "having no power to implement the demands of conscience, the concern for justice is transmuted into a distorted form of love, which, in the absence of justice, becomes chaotic self-surrender." The Churchmen were emphatic about the intention of the signatories to continue their concern for Black improvement despite the popular sentiment that "gains" already made in civil rights would be jeopardized. But they were also careful to disassociate themselves from the more radical and nationalistic elements by referring to America as "our beloved homeland." The document was signed by some of the country's most distinguished Black clergy, including several bishops and other high officers of the Church.[37]

At first the white Church recoiled in disbelief, and many Black churchmen were uncomfortable with such a forthright "political" statement. In the end, led by the National Council of Churches, white Christianity was moved to make its peace with the notion that the NCBC statement was a comparatively mild and reasonable statement of the new Black determination to be totally and responsibly involved in the life of America. The next communication from the Black community would be considerably more shocking and not nearly so easy to live with.

The National Committee of Black Churchmen established a permanent headquarters at the Convent Avenue Baptist Church in Harlem. Its formal organization was perfected at a conference in Dallas,[38] and it soon became a factor in the development of "Black caucuses" in every major white denomination. Beyond that, the organization soon became recognized as that representation of the Black Church with which non-Church dissidents and radicals could communicate most effectively. It was through this agency in its role as a Black Church contact with America's more disaffected Blacks that James Forman made some very controversial history at Manhattan's Riverside Church. Forman, once prominent in the leadership of SNCC but more recently eclipsed by the political flamboyancy of Stokely Carmichael and H. Rap Brown, was able and experienced in civil rights strategy.

After four years in the military he had interrupted his graduate studies at Boston University for a more immediate involvement in the civil rights struggle. He helped organize the Black farmers in Brownsville, Tennessee, who had been forced off the land in reprisal for their voting activity. Later he succeeded Bob Moses as director of SNCC's famous Mississippi Project. Although considered "radical" and "Marxist," Forman enjoyed a close working relationship with the Black Church and had gained the respect of most of the Black clergy involved in civil rights activity. He had participated in Martin Luther King's celebrated Selma, Alabama, campaign, and he was no stranger to the white power structure, its lawmen, and its jails.

For some time the Black clergymen associated with NCBC had been concerned about Black economic development as the next logical and necessary step in the ongoing freedom movement. The economic situation for a small segment of the Black minority had improved, but for the Black masses the economic gap between them and the rest of America was actually widening. Worse, the progress of the few Blacks who could be pointed to was in most cases linked to their willingness and ability to accept subservience to whites who dictated conditions from secure positions of power. This was progress in a vacuum. Nowhere were Black people able to make their own decisions, determine their own values, and still survive with dignity. White power remained the arbiter of Black survival.

In late April 1969 the Interreligious Foundation for Community Organization (IFCO) sponsored a Black Economic Development Conference at Detroit's Wayne State University. The official relationship between NCBC and IFCO has not always been clear, but it is clear that they vibrated with a certain sympathy born of interlocking memberships and a common experience with the white Church Establishment.[39] In any case, Forman, who was not a member of either organization (but who was ultimately supported by both), appeared at the Conference and read a startling "Black Manifesto," which was approved by a majority of the delegates as the consensus of the Conference.[40]

The preamble of the manifesto was written by James Forman himself. Severely Marxist in tone, it denounced American capitalism and imperialism and announced the intention of "building a socialist society inside the United States." Such a society would be led by Blacks but would be "concerned about the total humanity of this world." Blacks who support capitalism were labeled "black power pimps and fraudulent leaders . . . contributing to the continuous exploitation of black people all around the world." Forman referred to the United States as "the most barbaric country in the world" and spoke of "revolution, which will be an armed confrontation and long years of guerrilla warfare in this country." Once Blacks are in power, whites would have to accept Black leadership, "for that is the only protection that black people have . . . from [white] racism. . . ." Blacks were urged to "think in terms of total control of the United States. Prepare . . . to seize state power."

The text of the manifesto was considerably more restrained but no less startling. It referred to the centuries during which Blackamericans "have been forced to live as colonized people inside the United States" and demanded of "the white Christian churches and Jewish synagogues, which are part and parcel of the system of capitalism, that they begin to pay reparations to black people in this country." The manifesto demanded a total of $500 million from the white churches and synagogues, calculated at "fifteen dollars per nigger." It elaborated a schedule for expenditure of the money which included a land bank for evicted Black farmers in the South, publishing and printing industries, television networks, assistance to welfare recipients, a research center, training centers, a Black university, and other benefits of a public nature for Blacks. It appealed to "all black people throughout the United States" for support and called for the "total disruption of selected [white] church-sponsored agencies operating anywhere in the United States and the world." Church properties seized were to be held in "trusteeship" until the demands of the manifesto were met.[41]

The following Sunday Forman strode into Riverside Church, interrupted the worship service then in progress, and read the "Black Manifesto" from the pulpit. For weeks thereafter Western Christendom reverberated with the shock waves of the incident. Although Riverside's pastor, Ernest Campbell, and two-thirds of the worshippers left the sanctuary at Forman's intrusion, Dr. Campbell's statement of response proved him to be one of the few white Church leaders able to see the issues that lay beyond Forman's personal rhetoric and sacrilegious tactics. Said Dr. Campbell:

> Let's be done with rationalizing. Wherever you go in this country the white man rides higher than the black. He lives in better parts of town, sends his children to more desirable schools, . . . holds down better paying jobs. In . . . Vietnam, more blacks are dying because the draft laws that prevail favor white youth. . . .
>
> And where has the Church been in all of this? By its silence it has blessed these arrangements and given them an extra area of divine approval.[42]

Dr. Campbell then addressed himself directly to the issue of reparations, an issue most Church leaders either ignored, evaded, or otherwise declined to come to grips with:

> Reparations, restitution, redress, call it what you will. We subscribe to the conviction that given the demeaning and heinous mistreatment that black people have suffered in this country at the hands of white people in

the slave economy, and given the lingering handicaps of that system that still works to keep the black man at a disadvantage in our society, it is just and reasonable that amends be made by many institutions in society—including, and perhaps especially, the church. . . .[43]

The response of the white Church can be summed up as both varied and confused.[44] Most official statements deplored racism and pointed to programs they already sponsored, or intended to sponsor, to reduce the effects of racism and alleviate poverty. They were prepared to expend funds through existing machinery within their own establishments, or through the Urban League, or through Black caucuses within their own denominations, or even through NCBC. But they were not willing to concede the principle of reparations, or recognize James Forman, or hand any money over directly to the Black Economic Development Conference. The Jewish groups seemed particularly antagonized by the idea of reparations, and Jewish representation on the Board of IFCO was withdrawn.[45]

The "Black Manifesto" is probably not one of the great documents of history, but as Prof. Charles V. Willie has put it, "the prophetic comes to us sometimes in preposterous wrappings." The "Black Manifesto," said Willie, "presented us with the uncomfortable task of sorting out the meaningful from the foolish." [46] But the manifesto did more than that: it placed a *miroir noir* before the conscience of American Christianity and forced it to look at its own blemishes. What was seen was not complimentary to the faith.

The critical accomplishment of the "Black Manifesto," though, was that its promulgation showed the world yet once again the contingent relation thirty million Blackamericans must endure in respect to white Americans—and it gave fair warning of the dangers inherent in so anomalous a situation. The voice of prophecy is seldom welcome at the dinner table, and for Black America it often seems that white America never gets up from the table . . . never has time to listen. This is possibly what Father Junius Carter, Black rector of the Holy Cross Episcopal Church, was saying when he addressed the bishops of his church:

Too long, bishops, you have sat on the sidelines and have not acted as our pastors! I urge you to . . . exercise the authority which has been given you by our Lord. . . . You've talked about black brotherhood, but forget it, Joe. You don't mean it. . . . It's nothing but a damn lie. You don't trust me, you don't trust black priests and you don't trust black people. You keep saying, "Be calm, be patient," I'm sick of you. . . . To hell with love! [47]

The Black Church has not yet reached the regions of despair plumbed by Father Carter, but his may be a voice crying in a crowded wilderness. The Church may be ordained of God, but it is a creature of society. As such, the needs and aspirations of the people who comprise it may be read in much of what the Church does, or refuses to do. Presently, the determination of Black people for responsible participation in the full spectrum of life in America will continue to be reflected in an aggressive Black Church. The presence of power is the absence of contingency, the sign of responsibility, of order and meaning in life. The Black Church has learned something of how power is acquired and how it may be expended to best effect. Power in the United States begins with the "E" of economics. In times past the lodges and fraternal orders of the Black Church sought to cope with the economic deprivation of its people. Today the Black Church in Atlanta and Boston has put its money into apartments for the poor—its prevailing membership. In Philadelphia and Chicago, jobs for the people and training for the jobs mark the impact of the Church. Everywhere—in New York and Dallas and California, the Black Church has broken free from the chrysalis of accommodation. By proclamation, by manifesto, by caucus, and by deed it is trying to communicate with Christian America, to tell the good news of its self-liberation.

3

THE NEW
BLACK THEOLOGY:
ITS MEANING
AND ITS RELEVANCE

A Black theology is the logical expression of a mature design for liberation. The classical Church is a conservator of values, which means that it vests its interests in the status quo. But the Church *can* be aroused, and the Church militant is a force before which few institutions can stand. Marx was only half right: religion may be the opiate of the people, but religion is also a combustible that has been known on no few occasions to make the most significant changes in the course of human history. Religion is alike the nurture and the narcotic of civilization. Nations have been raised in its name, and nations have slipped into oblivion through its narcotism. Vast numbers of people have accepted slavery, pariah status, and even death in response to the demands of the faith they lived by, and there are occasions in history when religious faith has been a flaming sword of liberation.

Black religion is self-consciously committed to the detruction of caste in America and is moving quite visibly in some instances, less perceptibly in others, toward the principle that Christian commitment is inconsistent with powerlessness and lack of freedom. As "white" theology has always functioned as the intellectual expression of American Christianity, the advent of Black theology must be read as the determination of the Black Church to reinforce its commitment to liberation. The times are propitious: the Black

Church has a more sophisticated laity than ever before; the mood of Black consciousness crosses all denominational and class lines and erases altogether or at least clouds some traditional distinctions (such as color) which have fragmented Black togetherness; for the first time, the whole white Church is under suspicion, and the white Church no longer represents the model toward which significant numbers of Black Christians aspire. But perhaps more important than anything else is that for the first time the Black Church has the available intellectual resources to engage in a serious theological debate, and to construct for itself a theology consistent with its needs. While the Black Church has traditionally been the nurture as well as the beneficiary of Black scholarship, relatively little of that talent has been previously directed toward establishing the theological independence of Black religion. The Black scholars who have addressed themselves to the religious enterprise have for the most part been content to accept both the premises and the parameters laid down by their white Christian mentors, with predictable results. That has changed. The last decade has produced an ever-widening cadre of able Black scholars with superior credentials who are willing to look for truth beyond the bounds their masters knew. Black theology emerges as a phenomenon of the times. It is the religious aspects of the Blackamerican's quest for meaning, for relevance, and for justification in an America which has hardly recognized his presence.

The theological enterprise begins properly with a careful definition of terms. Thus, "theology comes from two Greek words," we are told, *theos*, meaning "God," *logos*, meaning "word," or "rational thought." "Therefore," declares Prof. William Hordern, "theology is a rational thought about God." [1] Vergilius Ferm in his *Encyclopedia of Religion* extends the dimensions of theology significantly when he defines it as "the discipline which concerns God (or the Divine Reality) and God's relation to the world." [2] Ferm's elaboration is crucial because it relates God to history and opens up the possibility that He is engaged, or may be engaged, in the affairs and the concerns of men. David Wesley Soper says that not only is theology bread for men hungry for meaning, but it is also "pure water and strong wine" to men "athirst in the Sahara of modern meaninglessness." "Modern man faces two alternatives," says Soper, "meaning or madness. Therefore, theology must speak not only about the meaning which man creates, but primarily about the meaning and the mystery which have created, and are now creating man." [3]

All this seems to suggest that theology is critical to man's understanding of himself, his world, his place in the world, and whatever *Power* there is to which man and his world must answer. To be, to exist at all, is to exist in a context of relationships by which one's existence is defined and explicated. This, it would seem, requires every man to be in some sense a "theologian," i.e., to have some rational thoughts about God, himself, and the circumstances of his being. It is probable that theology presupposes religion.

Religion is never incidental to the culture, and every theological formulation, no matter how primitive, no matter how sophisticated, must ultimately be seen against the culture that produced it, if such a theology is to be understood. Existence is prior to essence (in this instance the existentialists are right!), and it may be said with confidence that a universally relevant theology has yet to be written, and indeed cannot be written in the absence of a common cultural experience. The crucial task of the theologian is to assist the religious practitioner in the critical business of making sense of experience—his own experience first of all, and secondarily his vicarious experiences, i.e., the meaningful experiences of others which have been, or which are capable of being, incorporated into the framework of reality as the practitioner has encountered it. To argue that theology deals with what is ultimate and transcendent and must therefore address itself to a universal community is to ignore the most obvious fact of human existence, i.e., man's finitude—his limited experience and his incapacity to broaden that experience into a universal norm. True, man can project himself through his ideas—his reasoning, his imagining, his understanding, his believing. Theology makes its appeal to all of these. But the understanding, too, is shaped by experience, and the richest imagination cannot re-create the real with absolute fidelity. So we rely on symbols to take over where reality leaves off, and the language theology knows best is a language in which symbols take on impressive tasks of communication. The symbols change their meaning, and words lose their definitions in the transcendental effort. The new words and symbols, the new definitions for old words confuse and sometimes outrage rather than inform.

In many quarters, "Black theology" is itself dismissed as presumptuous, preposterous, impertinent, or improbable. But once dismissed, it does not obligingly self-destruct for those who happen to be disturbed or offended by it. It must be considered. It must be dealt with because it raises critical issues germane to any reasonable understanding of the faith—issues which other contemporary theologies have chosen to ignore. Black theology may itself be ignored in its turn, but Black theology by its very nature presumes and exposes white racism, and the issue of racism is going to become increasingly critical to the life and relevance of American Christianity. It is not going to oblige theological conviviality by restricting itself to the secular mode. Hence, Black theology is in some sense an invitation to contemporary white theologians to address themselves to the hard problems of God's role in the contemporary human situation. The chancre of racism has been wasting the Church in America, in ways too devious to be happenstance, too obvious to be overlooked, and Black theology may turn out to be the challenge that rescues the faith from its moral inertia. Indeed, it may well give those who like to speak of "doing theology" some relevant theology to do! It may be the answer to the theology of benign neglect—the theology which has operated on the principle that the white man's understanding is sufficient and proper for all men and all conditions of man and that the Black man's understanding could be improved by leaving him conveniently alone.

Every society has a religious involvement, and religion is a social institution. While at the personal level theology may be the insight of Everyman, nevertheless it must also become in its fullest expression the normative insight of the group, i.e., the collectivity for which it functions as a clarifier of religion and the magnifier of religious values. It remains a personal enterprise only in the same sense that Everyman practices enough medicine to cure his simple ailments

without being a physician or understands the simple relationship of numbers without being a mathematician. This is
not to say that an "official" theology is ever agreed upon by
ballot, or that there will never be dissent from whatever
becomes the group norm of theological understanding. It is to
say, however, that dissent becomes heresy or heterodoxy
precisely because it is in conflict with settled opinion and
social consensus and is for that reason perceived as a threat to
the socio-theological norm of understanding about God and
man, man and man, and man and God.

Prof. William Hordern tells us that "theology must hang
together [developing] systems of thought in which the answer
given to one question throws light upon the next." [4] And
Edwin Lewis declares that "the life process is a process of
self-realization, determined solely from within, although
contingent on the nature of external condition." [5] If the
question of theology as an "official," institutionalized
clarification of man's religious experience has remained to
this point unresolved, Hordern's statement should be finally
instructive. The layman does not construct systems of
thought which "hang together" as rational discourses about
God and man in a way in which "the answer to one question
throws light upon the next." That is the task of the professional theologians, scholars who offer the authoritative
clarification of religion and the magnification of its values
upon which the faithful may depend for "pure water and
strong wine" when they are "athirst in the Sahara of . . .
meaninglessness." "The need for security," says Reinhold
Niebuhr, "is a basic need of human life." [6] If that is true, then
theology is a critical component of man's security system, and
the professional theologian is, in a community of believers, a
critical influence on social understanding and social behavior.
If, as Edwin Lewis contends, life has to do with self-realization—a process he claims to be determined "solely from
within," though conditioned by externals, then man's perception of himself, his God, his neighbor, and the world
around him constitutes the nexus by means of which his sense
of reality is shaped.

There are those who are willing to contend that, until the
advent of the brothers Niebuhr and the Americanization of

Paul Tillich, there was no American theology and that there is little theology of any consequence being written in America today. One well-known American theologian once suggested to another that "there is no American theology" and admitted that he, like most other American theologians, had been "exclusively preoccupied with European theologians, ancient, medieval and modern." 7 American theology, he discovered, was still in its adolescence. No doubt he was right—if his reference was to the absence of a mature humanitarian conceptualization in American theological thought. But if he was referring to the power of American theology to influence social policy or to set the tone for social relations in a democracy consciously and officially conceiving itself to be a society "under God," the conclusions offered do not necessarily follow. There *is* an American theology. And there *has been* an American theology for more generations than are necessary for thought to mature and concepts to refine themselves. There *is* and there *was* an American theology, but it is and it always has been a theology singularly lacking in its ability to conceive of humanity beyond the improbable boundaries of the white race. It has always been a theology which permitted and sometimes encouraged the sickness of racism and which has on occasion grossly distorted the faith through a calculated attempt to fit the whole of reality into the narrow confines of a doctrine of racial expediency and a deep-seated commitment to a racial manifest destiny. If it is to this act of religious and intellectual obscenity that reference is made when American theology is called "adolescent," then the criticism is in order, for American theology has yet to mature.

Despite the brashness held to be characteristic of our national spirit, the cultural umbilical cord which joins America to Europe is still intact. And since our cultural–intellectual establishment is a European derivative, we have always been inordinately dependent upon European inspiration and European ratification for standards of measurement of American cultural and intellectual achievement. This has been truer in theology and in philosophy than in any other interest, with the possible exception of art. Indeed, it has been as though Americans, separated as they were by the

Atlantic Ocean from European tutelage, could never develop either native proficiency or confidence in the humanities. Even to this day American theological trainees are "polished" by protracted study at European seminaries, and American seminaries are rated in terms of how many European theologians grace their faculties. There is nothing inherently wrong with this except that theology has to do with man in an existential situation, not in a hypothetical situation. It has to do with man's search for God and meaning where he is and in his time. Theology becomes relevant at the intersection of the activity of God and the activities of man in the context of history, and nowhere else. In consequence, European theology is essentially irrelevant to religion in America, and has been for a long time. It is irrelevant because, in the peculiar unfolding of her history, America developed peculiar institutions which required, but did not receive, theological attention of any consequence. There is in the United States a fully developed "American religion," which transcends denominational definitions and provides a common denominator for all of the American churches except the Black Church. That denominator bridges the gap between Protestantism and Catholicism in America, and it confirms the Pentecostals, the Mormons, the Christian Scientists, and the rest in a racial–cultural communion with the mainline denominations. There is nothing vital for European theology to say to American religion because American religion is a product of and the prime architect of the American experience, an experience unique in the history of Christendom. If American religion had been interested in a relevant theology, one which could speak meaningfully to the people in their own circumstances of existence, the search for illumination might well have begun at home.

The problem was and continues to be that American theology is so tainted with racial chauvinism as to be more obfuscatory than enlightening. Preston Williams, professor of theology at Harvard University, suggests that "Theology among Americans is wafer-thin. It may be adequate," he concedes, "but it is not profound." [8] Williams may be excessive in his charity. If American theology is "thin," it is because it has confined itself to being a "white tholeogy," an exclusivistic, irrational enterprise which has inevitably foundered over its refusal to come to grips with the white sin of Black slavery and its consequences. For this failure alone it must forfeit any claim to adequacy. Abraham Lincoln was so irritated by the theological evasiveness of his time, that he declared: "If the church would simply ask for assent to the Savior's statement of the substance of the law . . . 'thou shall love the Lord thy God . . . and thy neighbor as thyself,' that church I would gladly join." [9] In commenting on the strange, selective focus of white theology, Reuben Sheares II, a contemporary Black minister, explains:

> The role or status of Blacks in relation to the Gospel or white theology was that of an outsider—perhaps lower than that of a heathen or an infidel—as of one not covered nor included in its provisions. This is comparable to the status of Blacks under the Constitution. Its provisions simply did not apply to them. Consequently, Blacks were excluded from the moral and ethical protections of the Church and the faith. Blacks were set apart— beyond white theology. [10]

And Williams concludes that "The consequence of white racism is black distrust. Blacks simply cannot trust whites, their systems of truth or their institutions of society." [11]

If Black people cannot trust white people and their systems of truth, it is obvious that the white man (who is already preoccupied with the consequences of his whiteness), cannot create an acceptable theology for Black people. The white man's perspective is distorted by his values, and his values are centered around the color of his skin and the salience of his economics. That is a fact which was never lost on Blackamericans, even when they were in physical bondage. Lumsford Lane, a distinguished Black cleric who grew up in slavery once commented on the perplexing ambiguity of the Christian slavemaster:

> There was one hard doctrine to which we as slaves were compelled to listen, which I found difficult to receive. We were often told by the ministers how much we owed to God for bringing us over from the benighted shores of Africa and permitting us to listen to the sound of the gospel. In ignorance of any special revelation that God had made to master, or to his ancestors, that my ancestors should be stolen and

enslaved on the soil of America to accomplish their salvation, I was slow to believe all my teachers enjoined on this subject. How surprising, then, that this high moral end being accomplished, that no proclamation of emancipation had before this been made! [12]

As it was with the masters of the slaves, so it has been with the master theologians, who write learned treatises about theological dyspepsia and engage in endless dialogues about a fearsome variety of inanities. But their excursions around reality are as obvious as the hypocrisy of the slavemasters a hundred years ago. Dr. James Cone is one of a widening cadre of Black scholars who have addressed themselves to the task of understanding what is really happening in American theology. Cone defines the situation in this way:

it is evident that white American theology has served the oppressors well. Throughout the history of this country, from the Puritans to the death-of-God theologians, the theological problems emanating from the white churches and theological schools are defined in such a manner that they are unrelated to the problem of being black in a white racist society. By defining the problems of Christianity independently of the black condition, white theology becomes a theology of white oppressors, serving as a divine sanction for criminal acts committed against blacks. No white theologian has ever taken the oppression of black people as a point of departure for analyzing God's activity in contemporary America. Apparently white theologians see no connection between whiteness and evil or blackness and God.[13]

In the search for an understanding of the theological enterprise in America, it has seemed logical to look closely at the works of American theologians, but the examination of the works of one distinguished authority after another leads only to the discovery that most of them make no reference whatever to the racial situation in America, and those who do give it the shortest of shrift. It is as if Black people do not exist—indeed have never existed. Thus have America's theologians consistently avoided the most remarkable opportunity to be theologically relevant to the American situation. This pattern of avoidance suggests at least one of the reasons why Americans study theology in Europe. It is not unrelated to the reasons why we once sent missionaries all over the world while our domestic human relations were seriously close to a "state of nature"; or why we still pursue the romantic notion of "making the world safe for democracy" by dispensing our peculiar brand of social and political ethics in distant corners of the globe when democracy at home leaves so much to be desired.

The definition of an enterprise may be reasonably expected to set the parameters of discourse concerning it. In the case of theology as it is understood in America, some further elucidations or modifications are probably indicated. The definitions I have offered are the definitions of American theologians,[14] but what they have to say about theology is not altogether relevant to the American experience. "The problems which confront us today," Hordern declares, "did not leap suddenly into life in the twentieth century. They were generated by our past and cannot be understood apart from it." [15] Certainly this is true, but a functional definition of theology ought to leave room for the consideration of the problems Hordern tells us about.

The central problem is that white theology has excluded Black people from its universe of discourse and from its area of meaningful concern. In so doing, white theology has encouraged the notion that Black people are somehow beings of lesser consequence in the eyes of God, that they are not capable of proper Christian witness and that, being so limited, God does not require or expect very much of them. Implicitly, the white Christian is excused from the necessity to relate to Black people in terms of the full requirement of his Christian commitment, because Blacks are incapable of accepting and responding to such a relationship on terms of parity.

One of the classic strategies of racism is to deliberately organize social and personal perception in such a way that the practical oblivion of the proscribed subject is consistently accomplished. One need not take into account what one does not see, and what one does not see, for all practical purposes, does not exist. Practical invisibility, *oblivion,* is the common experience of Black people in a world dominated by whites. The practical invisibility of Blacks sustains the profane illusion that the world as presently ordered is the best available and encourages the self-elected shapers of human destiny to indulge the euphoria of fantasy. They want *not* to see Blacks who are hungry, Blacks who need housing, Blacks who for want of a modicum of power are always pawns, never players in the game. Racism always requires the prestidigitation of instant Blacks who will perform the nation's menial labor, or secure the nation's military presence in doubtful adventures in far-off places, or be the supporting cast for the nation's amusement or self-projection without complicating the arrangement by intruding their humanity. At all other times the common wish is for Black people to go away. To get lost. To vamoose. To vanish. And the strategies for Black disappearance, psychological and physical, constitute the principal agenda for the racist enterprise.

White Western theology has contributed significantly to the involuntary invisibility of Black people—to Black oblivion. The agony of the Black oppressed has not been heard. The travail of the Black masses has been ignored. Since theologically Black people do not exist, white theology has nothing to say to them about the purpose and meaning of their lives, and by this pretension it confirms white religion in its racial parochialism while consigning Black Christians to irrelevance. In sum, white theology is an entrapment that leaves the Black Christian without hope, without recourse, and without identity, and leaves white Christians with unrealistic views about themselves and about Christian responsibility. None of the hard questions about meaning or morality are answered. "Privileged groups," says Soper, "have habitually denied the under-privileged every opportunity to cultivate any capacity, and then ungallantly accused them of lacking what they had been denied the right to acquire." So with American theology. There can be no comfort in it for anyone who is Black, because it does not address itself to Black people.

Black theology is in some sense what is missing from white theology. To the degree that it fulfills its own best intentions, it is the restoration of a deficit incurred through the habitual malfunctioning of a racist calculus. Black theology is addressed to Black people. It arises from an appeal of the Black community to know itself and to know God in the context of Black history. It is the inevitable response to the anguished cry of a people who are trying to see themselves through new prisms of reality the better to know who they really are and what God's will for them may be in terms of that reality. Tradition has made God a party to their vilification and their denigration. White theology offers no rescue from this pit, no light in this darkness, so Blacks must write their own theology, and they will:

> Blacks are going to write American theology for the black church. It may be Christian; it may be Islamic; it may be atheistic. One thing seems certain: it will reflect upon the experiences of the black man and conclude how God acts in his world and what it means for the life of the black man. The black theologian shall proceed through blackness to humanity and God.[16]

White Christians will object, for white people always object when Black people make their own decisions. It will be argued that "Black theology" is absurd—as if America has ever known anything other than white theology, which by the same token must be absurd. But Black theology need not be absurd; it is an effort to make sense of the Christian faith for Black Christians, and if it succeeds in doing this, its contribution to the faith will be formidable. At least one Black theologian defines theology itself in a way that permits—even *requires* a Black expression. Dr. James Cone writes:

> In a society where men are oppressed because they are *black*, Christian theology must become *Black Theology*, a theology that is unreservedly identified with the goals of the oppressed community and seeking to interpret the divine character of their struggle for liberation. "Black Theology" is a phrase that is particularly appropriate for contemporary America because of its symbolic power to convey both what whites mean by oppression and what blacks mean by liberation.[17]

and

> Concretely, this means that black theology is not prepared to accept any doctrine of God, man, Christ, or Scripture which contradicts the black demand for freedom now. It believes that any religious idea which exalts black dignity and creates a restless drive for freedom must be affirmed. All ideas which are opposed to the struggle for black self-determination or are irrelevant to it must be rejected as the work of anti-Christ.[18]

In Cone's view Black theology is a theology of liberation. It is an account of God's righteous indignation loosing the bonds from Black people and demanding that they free themselves "by any means possible." A theology of liberation does not require violence, but neither does it deny violence as a legitimate instrument of freedom. Men belong to God, and no man who is in bondage to another is free to answer God if he must first answer to some other man claiming to be his master.

A man is not a thing—until he has lost his dignity; until he is no longer the image of God. Violence or nonviolence is irrelevant to whoever has already been dehumanized by want of compassion in another. To be human, to be a person, that is the principal thing; and to insist on being so regarded, that is the minimum responsibility a man owes himself, his aggressor, and his God. Violence can never be isolated from the universe of circumstances of which an overt act may be merely the physical climax of a progression of interest. Violence is not so much a physical act as it is the implementation of the determination to compromise the humanity of another. It is the extension of an act of will, and it may or may not end in any overt act of physical aggression. The most insidious violence is the violence of decisions that are inhumane, originating from motives that are corrupt, directed against people who are powerless and unaware. Liberation is the restoration of dignity, the negation of violence. But counterviolence may be its instrument when all other means are exhausted.

Black theology began with the first sermon preached by a Black slave to his brothers and sisters huddled together in some plantation swamp or forest. It was not a systematic theology which "hung together in rational patterns of thought," but it was even then a theology of liberation because it questioned the established contention that God willed the desecration of the human spirit by reducing a man to a thing. Prof. Lawrence Jones ventures the assertion that the Black theology of the slave period "did indeed have a folk quality . . . but in many ways it was more true to the Gospel than its more formally developed counterparts in white theology"—an assertion that needs no documentation. The early Black theology, says Jones, "was a church, or preached theology . . . marked by an immediacy and a personal relevance which points to its contemporary," [19] [counterpart]. Black spirituals abounded in theological implications stressing hope, heaven, faith, and redemption. When freedom came and Black Christians were finally able to establish their own churches, Black theology, as distinct from the white theological perspective, crept boldly out of hiding. It was not yet refined, polished, or consistently well reasoned, but it had the solidity of feeling and experience, and it became an important corrective to the distortions of reality Blacks had always had to contend with in their search for God and meaning. By the time of the Civil War, the various strands of theological thought which could be gathered from the spirituals, the itinerant preachers, and the settled clergy began to represent a persistent theme in Black religion clearly distinguishable from the prevailing American religion. It all added up to a suspicion that the white man's doctrine was contrived and that the white man's religion was a foil for the white man's economic and political interests.

Bishop Henry McNeal Turner of the African Methodist Church was probably the first Black clergyman of note to define God as black. Turner declared in a passionate address in 1898 entitled "God Is a Negro":

> Demented though we be, whenever we reach the conclusions that God or even Jesus Christ, while in the flesh, was a white man, we shall hang our gospel trumpet upon the willow and cease to preach. We had rather . . . believe in no God, or . . . believe that all nature is God than to believe in the personality of a God, and not to believe that He is a Negro.[20]

Turner went on to say that he favored emigration because

> as long as we remain among whites, the Negro will believe that the devil is black and that he favors the devil, and that God is white and that he bears no resemblance to Him, and the effects of such sentiment are contemptuous and degrading.[21]

Black theology is not necessarily a treatise on the color of God, but the nature of God as revealed through His color gradually became a principal theme of the theological interests of Blacks over the past hundred years, and is of critical concern today. The "color" of God could only assume importance in a society in which color played a major part in the determination of human capacity, human privilege, and human value. It was not and is not a question of whether God is physically black, but it is a question of whether a man who is black can identify with a white God and can depend on His love and protection. In the nature of the Black experience, if God is white, He must be associated with evil, with the enemy, and He cannot be counted upon to care for Black people.

One of the important features of the Garvey Movement of the Twenties was Marcus Garvey's contention that only a Black God could solidify the Black peoples of the world into a unified "Black Nation." He proclaimed for Black people everywhere *"One Aim! One God! One Destiny!"* Garvey named the Rev. George Alexander McGuire, an Episcopalian priest, to reorder the religious thinking of the three or four million Blacks who followed him, and McGuire promptly set up Endich, a seminary for the teaching of Black theology. He demanded that Blacks "forget the white gods! Erase the white gods from your minds," and in response, Black churches across the country ripped out the painting of blond, blue-eyed Jesuses staring down from the walls of their sanctuaries and painted over the windows featuring the heavenly experiences of the white elect. A reproduction of the Black Madonna and Child became a popular symbol of race consciousness in Black homes, and it was the standard subject of calendar art displayed in Black-owned barbershops, restaurants, and other public establishments. The traditional pastoral scenes featuring Jesus as a shepherd were suddenly populated with flocks of black sheep rather than the usual white ones and snuggled in the black bosom of a black Jesus was now a black Lamb!

Black people have always taken their religion seriously. For them religion is personal—almost tangible; it is never an abstraction disassociated from the here-and-now, the experiences that shape the life situations of real people who are suffering and dying and struggling against forces they don't understand. Black Christians have never learned to *rationalize* God; rather they *personalize* Him and include Him in their life situations. Hence, a Black God is not only logical—He is practical. He is logical because the real world as Black people experience it is divided between whites and Blacks, and since whites are the enemy, the oppressors, it is logical that any help for Black people cannot come from a white god. A Black God is practical because, if a white God can't help you, or won't help you, what good is He? If His image is represented by white people, why run the risk of deceit and disappointment?

The vast majority of all Blackamericans who confess any religion at all consider themselves Christians, and this despite the uncomplimentary history of American Christianity in its dealings with them. But even those Black believers outside Christian communion have been so repelled by the racist posture of the white Church and by the institutionalization of racist practices throughout the whole fabric of American life, that they have sought relief through nonwhite divinities. To thousands of his followers, Father Divine is "God." Such a notion becomes less ridiculous than it appears on its face when one stops to consider what Father Divine represents.* First of all, he represents security—protection from hunger, from need, and from a hostile, repressive society of white people. Further, he represents love—love in a society which commonly devalues and rejects people who are Black. Divine offers Black people somebodyness; he gives them names, tasks, and responsibilities to underscore his high appraisal. But most important of all, he represents identity. Beyond that, even forgetting his claims to divinity, Divine has accomplished feats not ordinarily associated with Blacks, especially the poor, powerless Blacks who constitute the bulk of his followers. Isn't Father a multi-millionaire? Didn't he punish the white judge who put him in jail by causing the judge to have a heart attack and die within three days? Didn't he feed tens of thousands of people, Black and white, from an apparently inexhaustible supply, for nothing—giving jobs to whoever wanted to work during the Depression, when not even the Federal government could do anything for the poor Black masses? Doesn't he get millions of dollars from wealthy whites who give it to him because *they* think he is "God"? And finally, despite the fact that he has accomplished all this, *he is black! He looks like his followers!* For the troubled and dispossessed Blacks who follow him, for people looking for reassurance about who they are and why, if Father Divine isn't God, in our kind of society it is easy to imagine that some might wish he were. But Black theology isn't really talking about Father Divine.

---

* Although he has been physically dead for a number of years, his followers continue to speak of him in the present tense.

The Black Muslims offer another interesting contrast to Black Christians wrestling with the impact of color on the meaning of their faith. Although practically all of them come from Christian families or traditions, not only do the Muslims reject Christianity and Christianity's God, but from the very beginning they conceived Allah, the Muslim God, to be a Black God. In fact, Allah is the "Supreme Black Man," the incarnation of the Black Nation of Islam.[22] The significance of all this seems to be that there is in our culture so strong an identification of a white god with white religion that Black people feel driven to make a cultural reconstruction of God the central effort of their religious dissent.

But Black theology isn't talking about the Black Muslims either, although the Muslims have fielded their own theologians and apologists.[23] In recent times, the rejection of white theology as an adequate structuring of the God-and-man-in-history relationship has found expression in the informal preached theology of most of America's leading Black preachers, from Howard Thurman to Adam Clayton Powell to Martin Luther King, as well as in the formal writings of professional Black theologians. This countervailing Black theology has oftentimes been expressed by subtle means and often by careful innuendo, but the message is always clear to the Black believers. They have a long tradition of listening with the third ear, and hearing what is meant for their ears alone. In Muslim circles, Elijah Muhammad, the late Malcolm X, Louis Farrachan, and other articulate spokesmen have never muted their insistent message of a Black God for Black people with Black religion. In Christian circles, Albert Cleage of the Shrine of the Black Madonna is well known for his militant leadership in civil rights, and for his unrestrained preaching on the "Black Messiah." For Cleage, the liberation of Black people is both futile and meaningless unless they can identify with the Agent of Liberation.

It has been argued that America has produced no great theologians. If the argument holds, it is because the American theologians have characteristically shied away from the prophetic task of speaking the truth—the whole truth. They have too often "drowned their virtue in a silver cup, and sold their reputations for a song" of approbation. It is possible that we have entered an era of rectification. Yet, if Black theology is to be anything more than a countermyth and a more extravagant fiction, it will avoid at all costs the disparagement of principle and of the notion that the whole will of God is discoverable in one momentary event, or one set of relations. The wheel turns but always around the same axis, no matter what point of the perimeter is in momentary contact with the ground. Similarly, while the course of human events and the nature of human relationships are subject to change, the relation of God to man remains constant. It is this certainty that man can build on. Black theology, like every other theology, sees through a glass but darkly, and in part. It is the theology of the Black experience, a point in time on the circumference of that greater vastness, the whole human experience, of which God is always at the center.

4

THE NATION OF ISLAM: AN ALTERNATIVE EXPRESSION OF BLACK RELIGION

DURING the whole period of the Black man's sojourn in America there has been little challenge to Christianity as a religious way of life. While for the first hundred years there was little effort to Christianize the Africans brought here as slaves, the practice of native (African) religions was rigidly proscribed. In the interest of security, every effort was made to separate those slaves from a common tribal group or with a common language or religion. Since religion is sustained by a *cultus* which preserves and transmits the faith from one generation to another, the possibility of a diversified body of Africans of differing languages and religions carrying on a mature, "common" religion under conditions of American slavery was quite remote. There were very probably some African survivals incorporated into the patterns of belief and worship which came in time to be the Black Church, but what was "originally" African, and what was similar to African patterns but derived from other sources, and what has been reappropriated from the African past has not been delineated with certainty.

What is certain is that for all practical purposes most second-generation African slaves had little knowledge of and less opportunity to preserve any African religion. What is more, until the Society for the Propagation of the Gospel in Foreign Parts began its work among Blacks in 1701 (after proving unsuccessful with the Indians), there was little opportunity for the African diaspora to come in contact with *any* religion, except for those who escaped and were adopted into one of the Indian tribes.[1] The point is that, until quite recently, Christianity has been the only religious option available to Blacks in America. Even after America emerged as a world power, our exclusionist immigration policies, by very effectively keeping out Asians and Africans, kept America overwhelmingly "Judeo-Christian." Since Jews are not a proselytizing communion, few Blacks have considered Judaism as an attractive alternative to Christianity, although some Black Jews in this country claim a religious ancestry independent of American Jewry.

It is possible that some slaves brought to this country were Christian. It is probable that significant numbers were Muslim, as large portions of the areas which supplied the slave trade had long been conversant with Islam.[2] Hence, it is one of the little ironies of history that ninety percent of those Blacks in America who have accepted some version of Islam have done so within the last two decades. Within the last ten years the Sunni branch of "orthodox" Islam has attracted an increasing number of Blacks in the world of sports and entertainment, but the total number of Sunni Muslims remains quite small. Of far greater impact has been the Nation of Islam, a kind of home-grown expression of the Islamic faith led by Messenger Elijah Muhammad.

The Black Muslim movement,[3] as the Nation of Islam is popularly known, is the most powerful and in terms of numbers by far the most attractive alternative religious communion that has ever been available to Blacks in this country. It has an inevitable appeal to Blacks who have difficulty with American Christianity because of its racism, and with the Black Christian Church because of its posture of accommodation. On the other hand, the Black Muslims themselves have adopted American capitalism with a vengeance, a matter that has produced considerable dissidence within their own ranks. Today's more militant Black youth often see Christianity and capitalism as the twin screws of white oppression, and within the Muslim movement at the very moment when Black Islam has reached its most

impressive level of power and acceptance, the restiveness of
the more dissident Young Muslims has become a recurrent
feature of the price of growth and relevance. That the faint-
hearted and those who let themselves become too comfortable too soon become part of the problem and have to be dealt
with, is a familiar tenet of contemporary Black militance, and
the impatient young Blacks of this generation in and outside
the Muslim movement chafe under the restraints taken for
granted by less volatile Black leadership. Occasionally,
impatience gives way to exasperation, and exasperation
sometimes signals the onset of madness. The Young Muslim
dissidents want the Black Muslim hierarchy to be more re-
sponsive to the priorities of the Black Revolution as it is perceived by contemporary Black youth. They want the
Muslims to clearly identify with the so-called Third World, a
task which may be difficult for a movement with such strong
puritanistic–capitalistic overtones.

The concern for racial solidarity and, to a lesser degree, for
identification with the Third World of underprivileged, un-
derdeveloped, ex-colonized nonwhite peoples is a persistent
theme within most organizations attractive to Black youth.
While the Muslims have always been race-conscious, they have
also been clannish—looking out for their own and viewing all
others with suspicion, if not disdain. In theory, "all Black men
are Muslims by nature." In practice, all Blacks have been
treated as *potential* Muslims. Now there seems to be a determination among some of the younger Muslims to slough off the
traditional insulation that has separated them from the other
members of the Black bereft, and to make common cause with
the disinherited, even across racial lines, so long as the lines are
not white. In the prisons and jails some Puerto Rican and
Spanish brothers have joined up and acknowledged Black
Islam.

The inevitable question has to do with the Muslim leader,
the Honorable Elijah Muhammad and what is happening at
the top inside the Nation of Islam. First, Elijah is still in charge,
but increasingly he must rely upon others for help in managing
the affairs of the Nation. A man who lives modestly in spite of
the growing wealth of his religious empire, Muhammad, now
nearing eighty, is also building himself a new mansion at the

cost of more than half a million dollars—possibly tomorrow's shrine of the Black Nation of Islam. He is also building one hundred or so dwellings for the more deprived elements of the Black community on the crowded South Side of Chicago. That is not all: in 1972 the "Messenger," as he is known to his followers, paid another four million dollars for the properties of a Greek Orthodox church to be used as the nucleus of a Black university the Muslims will build in Chicago. Also on his immediate agenda is a 200-bed hospital. "Our people need a hospital of their own in the worst kind of way," the Messenger says. Muhammad has numerous other projects going for him and the Nation of Islam: an ultramodern printing plant here, a few apartment houses and office buildings there; a half dozen farms in the Georgia–Alabama outback; a meat-packing plant; a private jet nestled down at Chicago's Midway Airport. Of the plane, Muhammad confesses humbly, "My followers, they let me use it." The fact is, Allah has favored the Black Muslims and prospered them under Elijah, a fact not lost on thousands of Black Christians who rub shoulders daily with the industrious Muslims, who when they were Christians, were often in jail or on the dole.

Elijah Muhammad's personal acceptance in the Black community has been far from universal; yet his influence in changing Black self-concepts and fostering Black pride among the masses has been unmatched by any individual since Marcus Garvey, for the Black Muslims were the vanguard of the new Black ethnicity. They were first to accept their blackness and turn it into an asset.

For a long time it could be said, "as Muhammad goes, so go the Muslims," but now there is trouble in the mosques. There is ferment and dissent even in Muhammad's "inner temple" in Chicago. The storied discipline of the Muslims has been fractured by dissidence and violence. The dissidents say that the prophesied Armageddon has been too long delayed or that its priority is being usurped by a growing materialism, which, it is alleged, becomes increasingly indistinguishable from the values of the white-oriented *Black bourgeoisie*, or even those of the white devils themselves. The wealth of the Nation is increasingly visible. In addition to his farms and office buildings and apartments, Muhammad presides over a vast conglomerate of restaurants, bakeries, grocery stores, clothing stores, fish markets, a small clothing factory, various service establishments, a printing plant worth one and a half million dollars, and *Muhammad Speaks*, a newspaper with almost twice the circulation of its nearest Black competitor. All this in the name of Islam. *Black* Islam.

It is the mosques themselves, "Muhammad's Temples of Islam," which constitute the real wealth and power of the Black Nation. Each mosque is presided over by a minister, who shares his temporal power with a Captain of the F.O.I.—the Fruit of Islam. Every mosque is an economic unit as well as a spiritual and educational institution, so the well-being of the Nation is obviously related to the success of each local mosque. The mosques raise most of the money for the national enterprises, for example. In a thank-you letter published in *Muhammad Speaks*, Raymond Sharrieff, Supreme (or National) Captain of the F.O.I., assured the faithful that:

> We, the Laborers and Followers here in Chicago, together with our great Leader and Teacher, the Most Honorable Elijah Muhammad, send many, many thanks to all of you for the immediate and open-hearted response to the Nation's call.
>
> Your gifts and loans to the Nation during this drive will go toward accomplishing the goals the Nation has set before itself. We cannot help but succeed when we work and strive in the Name of Allah and His Messenger! Let us all remember that Allah is the Great Rewarder. . . . There comes a time when we all must make a sacrifice—this is one of those times.

The sacrifices the Muslims are called on to make are not just financial. They are expected to sacrifice time and all other competing interests—and repair to the mosques three times a week. Social life outside of official Muslim activities is sharply curtailed, or nonexistent. Schools for the children must be staffed and maintained, the newspaper must be sold, and individual brothers must be helped in the construction, organization, and promotion of their small business enterprises. But the local mosque is first and foremost the center of Muslim unity. It is the place where the teachings of Elijah Muhammad are heard and interpreted as the sacred gospel which alone can save the Black people of America and restore them to their rightful place of consequence and dignity in the world. The word of Elijah Muhammad is second only to the holy writ of the Koran, and even that ordering is academic, for only Elijah (who was taught by Allah-in-Person) and his ministers (taught by Elijah himself) can properly interpret the Koran. According to a Muslim proverb, "Allah is the Best Knower." And after Allah, who but Elijah? As for the ministers who periodically journey to Chicago to sit at the feet of the Messenger and spend long hours in home study listening to his tapes and radio addresses, revelation is never complete and final. The Koran (and the Bible) may contain all the wisdom necessary, but the white devils never sleep. They never cease to refine and expand the "tricknology" by means of which they keep a jump ahead of the ignorant and unwary. But Muhammad is the perennial fountain from which flows the only reliable waters of wisdom for successful living in these days of temporary white hegemony. "The Messenger has big shoes," says Harlem Minister Louis Farrachan. "Who could fill them?" "How can you appoint someone to take my place," asks Muhammad, "when I did not appoint myself? God Almighty appointed me. You are foolish to play with God's mission and his Messenger. . . ."

That is Muhammad's answer to the pressure for change from inside the mosques. While he remains the unquestioned (though not unchallenged) leader, every mosque is of itself a satellite center of power, and the Nation of Islam is no stronger than its central authority. Any fragmentation of power, any disloyalty or "hypocrisy" which seriously threatens the Chicago power center cannot be tolerated if the Nation is to survive as a viable force based on the obedience, unity, and discipline that make it so different from other groups. That is why the defection of Malcolm X was of far greater consequence to the Black Muslim world than uninformed reason might have suggested. In the world of Islam, "submission" is the principal thing. Submission to *one* authority. Elijah Muhammad's. Hence, whatever his intentions, Malcolm's attempt to establish the rival "Muslim Mosque, Inc.," was seen by the Black Muslims not as *competitive*, but as *divisive*—a fracturing of preexisting unity and a refusal of one minister to continue in submission to the recognized leader. It is the disciplined acknowledgment of Muhammad's superior wisdom that invariably prefaces every significant Muslim utterance with "Mr. Muhammad teaches us . . ."; and it is the recognition of Muhammad's supreme authority that cautions even the most incautious dissidents to aim their indictments somewhere below the papal throne, never at Muhammad himself.

Those who predicted the imminent fall of the Nation of Islam with the departure of Malcolm X either misunderstood the ideological infrastructure of the movement or made the common mistake of equating charisma with control and popularity with power. The Nation of Islam may indeed fracture beyond recovery with the demise of Muhammad, but so long as he lives the probability of a successful coup involving a transfer of power and control is remote. The reason is simple—no one else in the movement enjoys, or has ever enjoyed, the quasi-divinity with which the person and the office of the Messenger are invested. His particular charisma is invested with the history and experience of the movement itself, needing nothing from outside the traditional frame of reference.

As with other religions, the logic of outsiders offers no clues to the realities perceived by the true believers. To undetermined thousands of Blackamericans, Elijah Muhammad is the "final Messenger" of Allah. The notion of finality is important: it means that there will be no more reprieves. Blacks must get themselves together *under Elijah*, or they will forfeit forever the chance for cultural and spiritual, economic and political restoration. To the faithful, Muhammad alone is the man who walked with and was instructed by God. God ("whose right and proper name is Allah") gave Elijah his Muslim name and gave him the divine commission to resurrect "the mentally dead, so-called Negroes," and prepare them for Armageddon.

The key to understanding all Black Muslim behavior, as well as to understanding the attraction and popularity of Islam in the Black community, lies in understanding how Black Islam came to be. It began with the mysterious Master Wali Fard Muhammad who appeard in the Black ghetto of Detroit in the early Thirties. Fard, it is believed by the Muslims, came from the Holy City of Mecca for the express purpose of identifying and reclaiming the Lost Tribe of Shabazz—the Black Muslims in America who had been taught to think of themselves as "Negroes." Fard began teaching "the knowledge of self" and preparing the Lost Nation for a manifest destiny that had been temporarily deflected by the white man's momentary bubble in the flux of human history. In the Detroit of the early Thirties, racial hostilities were no less extravagant than they are now, but the plight of the Blacks there was somewhat more anxiety-producing if only because of a more degraded sense of self-identity and a hopelessly limited spectrum of options for meaningful involvement in American life. One of the more positive aspects of the Black Muslim movement is that, as it gathered momentum in the Fifties and Sixties, it compelled Black people to take a fresh look at their cultural and political priorities and experience the agony of reassessing those priorities in view of changing circumstances in America and the world. They needed to determine whether what they believed in was still relevant, and whether the goals they had set for themselves or had had set for them by others were likely to be realized in the reasonable, foreseeable future. Many Blacks did not like what they saw when they saw themselves in the mirror of contemporary times. They were ready for change. Some were ready for any kind of change. By any means necessary. That is in part the story of Martin Luther King, James Farmer, the Black Panthers, the Black Muslims, and other individuals and organizations who were involved in the struggle to undo what was and create what they hoped could be.

In the Thirties life was difficult for most Americans, whatever their race or color. For Blacks in the ghettoes of the North, the difficulties were compounded, for in the best of times their circumstances were precarious. Long before the white people recognized a "depression," many Blacks had already lost their jobs to the returning white veterans of World War I and were themselves depressed to the point of hopelessness. Competition for housing had become intense, and frequently it was violent. Black people had few victories to cheer them. When the big layoffs of the Great Depression finally came, Black workers were the first to go, as a matter of course. Many returned to the plantations of the South—from which they had been lured by the promise of good wages and good houses during the boom

years of the War. Those who stayed frequently ran the risk of
starvation or worse. Cases of freezing to death were not unknown and are still vivid in the folklore of Blackamerica. Those
on the dole found the minor agents of government who were
responsible for food distribution often hostile, vituperative,
punitive, and invariably, white. The self-esteem of the
struggling, starving Blacks in the ghetto quickly reached its
nadir. It had never been what could be called "vigorous," but
the bright promise of the North as a place where a man could
be a man and where, if the white man could make it, the Black
man could make it, too—if he'd hustle—had flared feebly for a
little while. Now it had winked out, and hope died with the
flame. But suddenly, out of nowhere, entered Wali Fard, the
Great Mahdi, who came as Allah-in-Person to those who
would believe, bringing with him the "knowledge of self,"
which is the supreme Black power—the only power adequate to
deal with the white man.

Like most saviors with claims of divinity, Fard's origins were
and remain obscure, which is to say, in religious terminology, a
"mystery." For the faithful, it is sufficient that he came *when* he
came and *for what* he came. Whence he came and to where
he departed to are of no consequence, for Deity is not a captive of any place at any time. At first Master Fard was
known simply as "The Prophet." His fame grew, and in three
years of teaching from house to house in the Black ghetto of
Detroit, he was able to convince a sizeable number of Blacks of
their divine ancestry—which they had never before suspected
—and of their natural religion, which is to say, Islam, when
they had always thought they were properly Methodists or
Baptists. He taught them, too, that they were the descendants
of a great civilization and that the white man is "a devil by
nature"—absolutely incapable of living with anyone who is not
white. The white man, said the Prophet, is the natural enemy
of all Black people, just as the hawk is the enemy of every bird
that flies. The hawk will even attack the eagle, if he finds the
eagle on its back. But when the eagle screams and spreads his
wings, the hawk flees for his life. Similarly, there must be a day
of reckoning between Black and white. It is the Battle of Armageddon promised in the Book of Revelation, when the forces
of evil will contend with the forces of good and be destroyed.[4]

Allah himself will insure a Black victory. In the meantime, all faithful Muslims will obey the law, submit to all "constituted authority," and live in peace with all who will live in peace with them. They must not arm themselves, but they must learn to protect themselves without weapons. The white man's dependence upon his weapons is his chief weakness, Fard taught. His weapons will be the instrument of his destruction. Echoes Elijah Muhammad, "The devils want you to carry weapons so that they can justify killing you. Allah has all the weapons you will need." Each Muslim is pledged to come to the defense of any other Muslim, even at the peril of his own life or safety. He is forbidden to initiate violence, but he is not required to walk away from it.

As Malcolm X once counseled the thousands of cheering Black youths who knew him as the chief expositor of Muhammad's Black Islam: "Never be the aggressor; never look for trouble, *but if any man molests you, may Allah bless you!* If the white man comes to take advantage of you," Malcolm exhorted, "*lay down your life!* And the whole Planet Earth will respect you." However, meaningful survival called for more than a proficiency in physical self-defense. It required a knowledge of how to make a living and a willingness to expend some effort in that interest. A viable Black nation meant an economically independent Black nation. If being black meant being last hired and first fired, Black people would have to create their own enterprises and their own jobs. If the white man could not be depended upon to share his abundance, Black people would have to create their own wealth. If Blacks were not welcome in the white man's schools, Blacks should build and staff their own schools and address their curriculum to the peculiar needs of the Black community. In short, Fard taught, "We must learn to do for self." Even the most uneducated Blacks knew how to farm. Why not pool their money and buy farms? Black domestics knew better than anybody how to cook, how to bake bread, how to sew. Why not open their own restaurants and bakeries and dress shops? A few Blacks had learned skills working for the white man. If each one should teach another the skill he knew, thereby creating a kind of skills bank for the whole Black Nation, "soon," said Fard, "we will again be our own architects and builders, and doctors and scientists, as well as farmers and laborers." But in the meantime, there were to be no class distinctions based on what one did for a living, and those who had to work for the white man were to "avoid exciting him, and deliver a full day's work for a full day's pay."

As a first principle of self-reclamation and survival, Fard taught the poor illiterates who invited him into their tumble-down tenements that they were *somebody*. That they were *Black people*. That they had a past, and that they had a future. They were people with a history and a destiny. If it seems that he was belaboring the obvious, one must be reminded that in the America of the Thirties, not all whites and practically no Blacks were automatically considered persons of consequence. Racism, elitism, and nativism reserved to a relative few the sacred right to simply "belong" without qualification. The hateful aphorism, "mighty few white folks and no niggers at all . . ." was a current expression of social class and racial exclusivism.

E. A. Ross, distinguished professor of sociology at the University of Wisconsin until 1937, could say confidently and publicly of certain European immigrants of the period that they were "hirsute, low-browed, big-faced persons of obviously low mentality . . . who clearly belong in skins and wattled huts . . . ox-like men who are the descendents of those who always stayed behind."[5] If that was the more learned perspective on immigrants, no extraordinary imagination is needed to reckon the estimate the masses of Americans less sophisticated than Dr. Ross had about Black people—who had been America's slaves! It was taught in the schools North and South to Blacks and whites alike that "Negroes have no history. They have never had a viable civilization." But Wali Fard taught *his* followers that they were the descendants of the ancient Black civilizations of Afro-Asia; of Black kings and Black warriors; Black scholars and Black scientists—lost children of a divine race, "first to inhabit the Planet Earth," and destined to be its final rulers.

The first step out of the morass of helplessness into which they had been cast by the white man's cupidity was to know the truth about themselves, said Fard. Knowledge of self is the first order of freedom.

Secondly, if the Black man is to realize the destiny willed

him by Allah—Black God of all Black people—then of course he must first survive. Survival means in the first instance recognition of the enemy—the white man. It means alertness and an unrelaxed defense against the inherent deviltry of the white man, whose "tricknology" assumes devious forms, all aimed at the reduction and the destruction of whoever is not white.

Fard disappeared in 1934, quite as mysteriously as he had come, and Elijah Muhammad took over the destiny of the Nation of Islam. Born Elijah Poole in Sandersville, Georgia, some 37 years before, he had dropped his "slave name" (Poole) when he attached himself to the Mahdi. Fard later gave him tl e Muslim name "Muhammad," in recognition of his hard work and dedication to the Cause. "Muhammad" means "praiseworthy." "The name," says Muhammad, "is everything." Having caught the mantle of leadership from Prophet Fard (who was later to be deified by the faithful as their "Savior"), Muhammad assumed the title "Messenger of Islam." For more than forty years since, he has been leader, teacher, and defender of his Black Nation, and he is the vicarious presence of the departed Great Mahdi. Fard is the Savior who came to rescue Black people and prepare them for the Armageddon, and "Savior's Day" is celebrated each year in February as the chief day of unity and preparedness. Elijah Muhammad is the Messenger who is charged with the completion of the task begun by Fard.

Along the way from the Georgia plantation where he was born, to the Black ghetto of Detroit, and finally to the development and leadership of the Nation of Islam, Muhammad learned something important about the vagaries of human existence, perhaps more especially of *Black* human existence. Both his parents had been slaves. When he arrived in Detroit in 1923, the racial backlash of the postwar era was already pronounced. It found expression in ten thousand experiences—overt and blatant; subtle and insidious; real and imaginary; experienced and anticipated. From all this, Muhammad says, "The Mahdi rescued me, and in three-and-a-half years he taught me Islam." It turned out that even Islam was no absolute haven from the usual slings and arrows of Black fortune. And Black leadership, then as now, had some built-in occupational hazards. As Messenger of Islam,

Muhammad was harassed by the police, badgered by the school board (he wouldn't send his children to public schools), scorned by the established Black leadership, hunted by a dissident faction of Muslims who wanted to assassinate him, and finally jailed by the Federal government on charges of sedition, conspiracy, and violation of the draft laws. His incarceration only heightened his stature among certain segments of the Black community. "I am the man," he announced. "I am not trembling. I am with Allah and He is with me." In prison at Milan, Michigan, Muhammad organized a Muslim cell group, and ever since then the prisons have been fertile sources of Muslim recruitment.

In 1932, in the face of intense internal factionalism and constant harassment from the outside, Muhammad managed to set up a second mosque, this time in Chicago. The Chicago mosque, now known as Muhammad's Temple of Islam No. 2, became the headquarters for the whole Muslim empire, which now stretches from Boston to San Diego, and from San Francisco to Miami. It is idle to speculate on how many Muslims these mosques represent. No one really knows. The Muslims are titillated by the opportunity to report that "Those who know don't say; and those who say don't know." Whatever their numbers, the Black Muslims are highly visible in the ghetto, and their leaders play an increasingly important role in ghetto affairs.

Despite Fard's emphasis upon racial awareness and the protection of Black people from white oppression, the essence of his teachings had to do with cultural identity, the acceptability and respectability of blackness, and economic self-help. These concerns are, of course, mutually reinforcing; and in the context in which they are given significance they do presume that white racial hostility is ultimately responsible for the basic insecurities to which Black people are subject. Hence the charge of counterracism is one that is frequently raised against Muhammad, for he has elaborated and refined the central doctrines of Fard into a politico-religious system which leaves no doubt about the identity and the fate of the enemy. In doing so, he has successfully transformed a sizeable segment of the Black poor and uneducated into an aggressive, confident, increasingly affluent Black Nation of Islam. His influence transcends religious and class lines and frequently touches people who do not recognize the source of what it is they find themselves affirming.

The ABC's of Elijah's Islam are quite simple: "Know yourself (and your kind); protect yourself (and your kind); do for yourself (and your kind)." It is a philosophy born of the Black experience in the ghettos of America, and while it is susceptible to the pitfalls of Black chauvinism, it was undoubtedly functional for the times and the circumstances which gave it birth. The degree to which it has remained both functional and attractive would seem to be a commentary on the rate as well as the degree of change in the options for meaningful Black survival in America. A decade ago, in an observation now classic for its perceptiveness at a time when most Black professionals dismissed the Muslims as just another lower-class embarrassment to the integration process, Edwin C. Berry, then Director of the Chicago Urban League, was moved to suggest that "to the man on the street getting his teeth kicked out, a guy like this Elijah Muhammad makes a hell of a lot more sense than I do. I have a sinking feeling that Elijah Muhammad is very significant." To the contemporary Black bereft whose sense of their mistreatment is finally focused on causative factors that have an origin beyond the ghetto and beyond their reach, the Muslims are, for the most part, still making sense, and Muhammad is eminently significant. Muslim prosperity approaches the conspicuous while other Blacks in the same ghetto and on the same block are treading water at best. At worst, they have succumbed to the implacable forces which first disdain, then distort, and finally destroy the lives of so many Americans whose original defect was no more than being born black but who wind up trapped by the inexorable consequences of that all-important attribute.

It must be obvious by now that being a Black Muslim has important implications for the believer himself, but no less for the society to which Elijah Muhammad's Black Islam is a deliberately calculated response. No part of the Muslim doctrine is incidental. From the dietary laws (one meal a day) to the prohibition of weapons, the Black Muslim program is a patterned response to what is perceived as a deliberate white offensive aimed ultimately at the removal or reenslavement of

Blacks. The rationale offered for what the Muslims do or do not do may or may not seem either rational or convincing, but as a system of survival in our kind of society the impressive evidence of its success is not lost upon the non-Muslim Black community.

The Black Muslims have come a long way since the critical days of the Thirties, and the respect and admiration they have garnered among the "so-called Negroes" in the ghettoes of America has been phenomenal in the last decade. Much of their program and many of their attitudes anticipated the restless disillusionment with white America that began in the early Fifties and ushered in the racial and political unrest we have all had to live with since. Our religious unrest is, of course, a projection of other anxieties and concerns that have gone unresolved. Murder, manipulation, and the most incredible scandals have strained our confidence in politics and government. The preoccupation with hedonistic values, the eclipse of the individual, the steady erosion of social control, the emergence of new, unorthodox life styles, and the loss of face and prestige in the international world have pushed the average American to the brink of his capacity to maintain social and personal equilibrium. The Blackamerican has his share of our common anxieties, but in addition he is still struggling for recognition and fulfillment at the very elemental level of personhood. We live in the Age of Now, and we are impatient with extended processes of "normative" social change. In the Black man's determination to recover and project an identity consistent with his sense of self, there would appear to be two viable alternatives. One is suggested by a well-known quatrain of the *Rubaiyat:*

> Ah Love, could you and I above with Him conspire
> To change this universe of things entire
> Would we not shatter it to bits
> And then remold it nearer to the heart's desire? [6]

The other would seem to be to opt for a religion ready-made for the time and for the circumstances. Black Islam promises instant identity and an established tradition independent of the white man's tampering or influence. The Nation of Islam has an economic program that works, and the evidence of its effectiveness is highly visible in the ghetto, where the Black masses have little to show or to hope for in terms of economic activity. The individual Muslims themselves are their own best currency of proselytism: they are clean, confident, prosperous, and respected. They are convinced that under a Black God they are building a viable Black Nation, and to this enterprise their total energies are committed. The problems of the white man's culture—alcohol, drugs, sexual deviation, family disorganization, juvenile deliquency, etc.—have been obviated by the strict puritanism of the Muslim code.

Such a religion for all its imperfections must inevitably attract many Black Christians grown weary and impatient with the peculiar conditions of Christianity in America. And it has, for there are no Black Muslims except those who left the Christian tradition in search of a more satisfying alternative.[7] The Black Muslims themselves see Islam as the Black man's logical progression from the way the white man taught to a faith that is his own. The traditional Black Church is not ready to go quite so far, but it has broken free of the mold that held it captive to its own contradictions. The contradictions are not resolved, and cannot be resolved so long as race is a significant determinant of Christian behavior. And since the prospects for a "raceless" church are not very pronounced, the Black Church would seem to have a continuing functional mission in the religious structure of America.

A

"BLACK POWER"

A STATEMENT BY THE NATIONAL COMMITTEE OF NEGRO CHURCHMEN

July 31, 1966*

WE, an informal group of Negro churchmen in America, are deeply disturbed about the crisis brought upon our country by historic distortions of important human realities in the controversy about "black power." What we see shining through the variety of rhetoric is not anything new but the same old problem of power and race which has faced our beloved country since 1619.

We realize that neither the term "power" nor the term "Christian Conscience" is an easy matter to talk about, especially in the context of race relations in America. The fundamental distortion facing us in the controversy about "black power" is rooted in a gross imbalance of power and conscience between Negroes and white Americans. It is this distortion, mainly, which is responsible for the widespread, though often inarticulate, assumption that white people are justified in getting what they want through the use of power, but that Negro Americans must, either by nature or by circumstances, make their appeal only through conscience. As a result, the power of white men and the conscience of black men have both been corrupted. The power of white men is corrupted because it meets little meaningful resistance from Negroes to temper it and keep white men from aping God. The conscience of black men is corrupted because, having no

* Nathan Wright, Jr., *Black Power* (New York, 1967), pp. 187–94.

power to implement the demands of conscience, the concern for justice is transmuted into a distorted form of love, which, in the absence of justice, becomes chaotic self-surrender. Powerlessness breeds a race of beggars. We are faced now with a situation where conscienceless power meets powerless conscience, threatening the very foundations of our nation.

Therefore, we are impelled by conscience to address at least four groups of people in areas where clarification of the controversy is of the most urgent necessity. We do not claim to present the final word. It is our hope, however, to communicate meanings from our experience regarding power and certain elements of conscience to help interpret more adequately the dilemma in which we are all involved.

I. To the Leaders of America: Power and Freedom

It is of critical importance that the leaders of this nation listen also to a voice which says that the principal source of the threat to our nation comes neither from the riots erupting in our big cities, nor from the disagreements among the leaders of the civil rights movement, nor even from mere raising of the cry for "black power." These events, we believe, are but the expression of the judgment of God upon our nation for its failure to use its abundant resources to serve the real well-being of people, at home and abroad.

We give our full support to all civil rights leaders as they seek for basically American goals, for we are not convinced that their mutual reinforcement of one another in the past is bound to end in the future. We would hope that the public power of our nation will be used to strengthen the civil rights movement and not to manipulate or further fracture it.

We deplore the overt violence of riots, but we believe it is more important to focus on the real sources of these eruptions. These sources may be abetted inside the ghetto, but their basic causes lie in the silent and covert violence which white middle-class America inflicts upon the victims of the inner city. The hidden, smooth and often smiling decisions of American leaders which tie a white noose of suburbia around the necks and which pin the backs of the masses of Negroes against the steaming ghetto walls—without jobs in a boom-ing economy; with dilapidated and segregated educational systems in the full view of unenforced laws against it; in short: the failure of

American leaders to use American power to create equal opportunity in life as well as in law—this is the real problem and not the anguished cry for "black power."

From the point of view of the Christian faith, there is nothing necessarily wrong with concern for power. At the heart of the Protestant Reformation is the belief that ultimate power belongs to God alone and that men become most inhuman when concentrations of power lead to the conviction—overt or covert—that any nation, race or organization can rival God in this regard. At issue in the relations between whites and Negroes in America is the problem of inequality of power. Out of this imbalance grows the disrespect of white men for the Negro personality and community, and the disrespect of Negroes for themselves. This is a fundamental root of human injustice in America. In one sense, the concept of "black power" reminds us of the need for and the possibility of authentic democracy in America.

We do not agree with those who say that we must cease expressing concern for the acquisition of power lest we endanger the "gains" already made by the civil rights movement. The fact of the matter is, there have been few substantive gains since about 1950 in this area. The gap has constantly widened between the incomes of non-whites relative to the whites. Since the Supreme Court decision of 1954, *de facto* segregation in every major city in our land has increased rather than decreased. Since the middle of the 1950s unemployment among Negroes has gone up rather than down, while unemployment has decreased in the white community.

While there has been some progress in some areas for equality for Negroes, this progress has been limited mainly to middle-class Negroes who represent only a small minority of the larger Negro community.

These are the hard facts that we must all face together. Therefore, we must not take the position that we can continue in the same old paths.

When American leaders decide to serve the real welfare of people instead of war and destruction; when American leaders are forced to make the rebuilding of our cities the first priority on the nation's agenda; when American leaders are forced by the American people to quit misusing and abusing American power; then will the cry for "black power" become inaudible, for the framework in which all power in America operates would include the power and experience of black men as well as those of white men. In that way, the fear of the power of each group would be removed. America is our beloved homeland. But, America is not God. Only God can do everything. America and the other nations of the world must decide which among a number of alternatives they will choose.

II.   To White Churchmen: Power and Love

As black men who were long ago forced out of the white church to create and to wield "black power," we fail to understand the emotional quality of the outcry of some clergy against the use of the term today. It is not enough to answer that "integration" is the solution. For it is precisely the nature of the operation of power under some forms of integration which is being challenged. The Negro Church was created as a result of the refusal to submit to the indignities of a false kind of "integration" in which all power was in the hands of white people. A more equal sharing of power is precisely what is required as the precondition of authentic human interaction. We understand the growing demand of Negro and white youth for a more honest kind of integration; one which increases rather than decreases the capacity of the disinherited to participate with power in all of the structures of our common life. Without this capacity to participate with power—i.e., to have some organized political and economic strength to really influence people with whom one interacts—integration is not meaningful. For the issue is not one of racial balance but of honest interracial interaction.

For this kind of interaction to take place, all people need power, whether black or white. We regard as sheer hypocrisy or as a blind and dangerous illusion the view that opposes love to power. Love should be a controlling element in power, but what love opposes is precisely the misuse and abuse of power, not power itself. So long as white churchmen continue to moralize and misinterpret Christian love, so long will justice continue to be subverted in this land.

III. To Negro Citizens: Power and Justice

Both the anguished cry for "black power" and the confused emotional response to it can be understood if the whole controversy is put in the context of American history. Especially must we understand the irony involved in the pride of Americans regarding their ability to act as individuals, on the one hand, and their tendency to act as members of ethnic groups, on the other hand. In the tensions of this part of our history is revealed both the tragedy and the hope of human redemption in America.

America has asked its Negro citizens to fight for opportunity as individuals whereas at certain points in our history what we have needed most has been opportunity for the whole group, not just for selected and approved Negroes. Thus in 1863, the slaves were made legally free, as individuals, but the real question regarding personal and group power to maintain that freedom was pushed aside. Power at that time for a mainly rural people meant land and tools to work the land. In the words of Thaddeus Stevens, power meant "40 acres and a mule." But this power was not made available to the slaves, and we see the results today in the pushing of a landless peasantry off the farms into big cities where they come in search mainly of the power to be free. What they find are only the formalities of unenforced legal freedom. So we must ask, "What is the nature of the power which we seek and need today?" Power today is essentially organizational power. It is not a thing lying about in the streets to be fought over. It is a thing which, in some measure, already belongs to Negroes and which must be developed by Negroes in relationship with the great resources of this nation.

Getting power necessarily involves reconciliation. We must first be reconciled to ourselves lest we fail to recognize the resources we already have and upon which we can build. We must be reconciled to ourselves as persons and to ourselves as a historical group. This means we must find our way to a new self-image in which we can feel a normal sense of pride in self, including our variety of skin color and the manifold textures of our hair. As long as we are filled with hatred for ourselves we will be unable to respect others.

At the same time, if we are seriously concerned about power, then we must build upon that which we already have. "Black power" is already present to some extent in the Negro Church, in Negro fraternities and sororities, in our professional associations, and in the opportunities afforded to Negroes who make decisions in some of the integrated organizations of our society.

We understand the reasons by which these limited forms of "black power" have been rejected by some of our people. Too often the Negro Church has stirred its members away from the reign of God in this world to a distorted and complacent view of an otherworldly conception of God's power. We commit ourselves as churchmen to make more meaningful in the life of our institution our conviction that Jesus Christ reigns in the "here" and "now" as well as in the future he brings in upon us. We shall, therefore, use more of the resources of our churches in working for human justice in the places of social change and upheaval where our Master is already at work.

At the same time, we would urge that Negro social and professional organizations develop new roles for engaging the problem of equal opportunity and put less time into the frivolity of idle chatter and social waste.

We must not apologize for the existence of this form of group power, for we have been oppressed as a group, not as individuals. We will not find our way out of that oppression until both we and America accept the need for Negro Americans as well as for Jews, Italians, Poles and white Anglo-Saxon Protestants, among others, to have and to wield group power.

However, if power is sought merely as an end in itself, it tends to turn upon those who seek it. Negroes need power in order to participate more effectively at all levels of the life of our nation. We are glad that none of those civil rights leaders who have asked for "black power" have suggested that it means a new form of isolationism or a foolish effort at domination. But we must be clear about why we need to be reconciled with the white majority. It is not because we are only one-tenth of the population in America; for we do not need to be reminded of the awesome power wielded by the 90% majority. We see and feel that power every day in the destructions heaped upon our families and upon the nation's cities. We do not need to be threatened by such cold and heartless statements. For we are men, not children, and we are growing out of our fear of that power, which can hardly hurt us any more in the future than it does in the present or has in the past. Moreover, those bare figures conceal the potential political strength which is ours if we organize properly in the big cities and establish effective alliances.

Neither must we rest our concern for reconciliation with our white brothers on the fear that failure to do so would damage gains already made by the civil rights movement. If those gains are in fact real, they will withstand the claims of our people for power and justice, not just for a few select Negroes here and there, but for the masses of our citizens. We must rather rest our concern for reconciliation on the firm ground that we and all other Americans are one. Our history and destiny are indissolubly linked. If the future is to belong to any of us, it must be prepared for all of us whatever our racial or religious background. For in the final analysis, we are persons and the power of all groups must be wielded to make visible our common humanity.

The future of America will belong to neither white nor black unless all Americans work together at the task of rebuilding our cities. We must organize not only among ourselves but with other groups in order that we can, together, gain power sufficient to change this nation's sense of what is now important and what must be done now. We must work with the remainder of the nation to organize whole cities for the task of making the rebuilding of our cities first priority in the use of our resources. This is more important than who gets to the moon first or the war in Vietnam.

To accomplish this task we cannot expend our energies in spastic or ill-tempered explosions without meaningful goals. We must move from the politics of philanthropy to the politics of metropolitan development for equal opportunity. We must relate all groups of the city together in new ways in order that the truth of our cities might be laid bare and in order that, together, we can lay claim to the great resources of our nation to make truth more human.

IV. To the Mass Media: Power and Truth

The ability or inability of all people in America to understand the upheavals of our day depends greatly on the way power and truth operate in the mass media. During the Southern demonstrations for civil rights, you men of the communications industry performed an invaluable service for the entire country by revealing plainly to our ears and eyes, the ugly truth of a brutalizing system of overt discrimination and segregation. Many of you were mauled and injured, and it took courage for you to stick with the task. You were instruments of change and not merely purveyors of unrelated facts. You were able to do this by dint of personal courage and by reason of the power of national news agencies which supported you.

Today, however, your task and ours is more difficult. The truth that needs revealing today is not so clear-cut in its outlines, nor is there a national consensus to help you form relevant points of view. Therefore, nothing is now more important than that you look for a variety of sources of truth in order that the limited perspectives of all of us might be corrected. Just as you related to a broad spectrum of people in Mississippi instead of relying on police records and Establishment figures, so must you operate in New York City, Chicago and Cleveland.

The power to support you in this endeavor is present in our country. It must be searched out. We desire to use our limited influence to help relate you to the variety of experience in the Negro community so that limited controversies are not blown up into the final truth about us. The fate of this country is, to no small extent, dependent upon how you interpret the crises upon us, so that human truth is disclosed and human needs are met.

Signatories:

Bishop John D. Bright, Sr., AME Church, First Episcopal District, Philadelphia, Pennsylvania

The Rev. John Bryan, Connecticut Council of Churches, Hartford, Connecticut

Suffragan Bishop John M. Burgess, The Episcopal Church, Boston, Massachusetts

The Rev. W. Sterling Cary, Grace Congregational Church, New York, New York

The Rev. Charles E. Cobb, St. John Church, UCC, Springfield, Massachusetts

The Rev. Caesar D. Coleman, Christian Methodist Episcopal Church, Memphis, Tennessee

The Rev. Joseph C. Coles, Williams Institutional CME Church, New York, New York

The Rev. Reginald Hawkins, United Presbyterian Church, Charlotte, North Carolina

Dr. Anna Arnold Hedgeman, Commission on Religion and Race, National Council of Churches, New York, New York

The Rev. R. E. Hood, Gary, Indiana

The Rev. H. R. Hughes, Bethel AME Church, New York, New York

The Rev. Kenneth Hughes, St. Bartholomew's Episcopal Church, Cambridge, Massachusetts

The Rev. Donald G. Jacobs, St. James AME Church, Cleveland, Ohio

The Rev. J. L. Joiner, Emanuel AME Church, New York, New York

The Rev. Arthur A. Jones, Metropolitan AME Church, Philadelphia, Pennsylvania

The Rev. Stanley King, Sabathini Baptist Church, Minneapolis, Minnesotta

The Rev. George A. Crawley, Jr., St. Paul Baptist Church, Baltimore, Maryland

The Rev. O. Herbert Edwards, Trinity Baptist Church, Baltimore, Maryland

The Rev. Bryant George, United Presbyterian Church in the USA, New York, New York

Bishop Charles F. Golden, The Methodist Church, Nashville, Tennessee

The Rev. Quinland R. Gordon, The Episcopal Church, New York, New York

The Rev. James Hargett, Church of Christian Fellowship, UCC, Los Angeles, California

The Rev. Elder Hawkins, St. Augustine Presbyterian Church, New York, New York

The Rev. Benjamin F. Payton, Commission on Religion and Race, National Council of Churches, New York, New York

The Rev. Isaiah P. Pogue, St. Mark's Presbyterian Church, Cleveland, Ohio

The Rev. Sandy F. Ray, Empire Baptist State Convention, Brooklyn, New York

Bishop Herbert B. Shaw, Presiding Bishop, Third Episcopal District, AMEZ Church, Wilmington, North Carolina

The Rev. Stephen P. Spottswood, Commission on Race and Cultural Relations, Detroit Council of Churches, Detroit, Michigan

The Rev. Henri A. Stines, Church of the Atonement, Washington, D.C.

Bishop James S. Thomas, Resident Bishop, Iowa Area, The Methodist Church, Des Moines, Iowa

The Rev. V. Simpson Turner, Mt. Carmel Baptist Church, Brooklyn, New York

The Rev. Earl Wesley Lawson, Emmanual Baptist Church, Malden, Massachusetts

The Rev. David Licorish, Abyssinian Baptist Church, New York, New York

The Rev. Arthur B. Mack, St. Thomas AMEZ Church, Haverstraw, New York

The Rev. James W. Mack, South United Church of Christ, Chicago, Illinois

The Rev. O. Clay Maxwell, Jr., Baptist Ministers Conference of New York City and Vicinity, New York, New York

The Rev. Leon Modeste, The Episcopal Church, New York, New York

Bishop Noah W. Moore, Jr., The Methodist Church, Southwestern Area, Houston, Texas

The Rev. David Nickerson, Episcopal Society for Cultural and Racial Unity, Atlanta, Georgia

The Rev. LeRoy Patrick, Bethesda United Presbyterian Church, Pittsburgh, Pennsylvania

The Rev. Edgar Ward, Grace Presbyterian Church, Chicago, Illinois

The Rev. Paul M. Washington, Church of the Advocate, Philadelphia, Pennsylvania

The Rev. Frank L. Williams, Methodist Church, Baltimore, Maryland

The Rev. John W. Williams, St. Stephen's Baptist Church, Kansas City, Missouri

The Rev. Gayraud Wilmore, United Presbyterian Church USA, New York, New York

The Rev. M. L. Wilson, Covenant Baptist Church, New York, New York

The Rev. Robert H. Wilson,

Corresponding Secretary, National Baptist Convention of America, Dallas, Texas

The Rev. Nathan Wright, Episcopal Diocese of Newark, Newark, New Jersey

(Organizational affiliation given for identification purposes only.)

B

THE BLACK
MANIFESTO*

TO THE WHITE CHRISTIAN CHURCHES
AND THE SYNAGOGUES IN THE
UNITED STATES OF AMERICA
AND TO ALL OTHER RACIST INSTITUTIONS:

*Introduction: Total Control as the Only Solution to the
Economic Problems of Black People*

Brothers and Sisters:

We have come from all over the country burning with anger and despair not only with the miserable economic plight of our people but fully aware that the racism on which the Western World was built dominates our lives. There can be no separation of the problems of racism from the problems of our economic, political, and cultural degradation. To any black man, this is clear.

But there are still some of our people who are clinging to the rhetoric of the Negro, and we must separate ourselves from these Negroes who go around the country promoting all types of schemes for black capitalism.

Ironically, some of the most militant Black Nationalists, as they call themselves, have been the first to jump on the bandwagon of black capitalism. They are pimps; black power pimps and fraudulent leaders, and the people must be educated to understand that any black man or Negro who is advocating a perpetuation of capitalism inside the United States is in fact seeking not only his ultimate

* Robert S. Lecky and H. Elliot Wright. *Black Manifesto* (New York, 1969), pp. 115–26

destruction and death but is contributing to the continuous exploitation of black people around the world. For it is the power of the United States Government, this racist, imperialist government, that is choking the life of all people around the world.

We are an African people. We sit back and watch the Jews in this country make Israel a powerful conservative state in the Middle East, but we are not concerned actively about the plight of our brothers in Africa. We are the most advanced technological group of black people in the world, and there are many skills that could be offered to Africa. At the same time, it must be publicly stated that many African leaders are in disarray themselves, having been duped into following the lines as laid out by the western imperialist governments. Africans themselves succumbed to and are victims of the power of the United States. For instance, during the summer of 1967, as the representatives of SNCC, Howard Moore and I traveled extensively in Tanzania and Zambia. We talked to high, very high, government officials. We told them there were many black people in the United States who were willing to come and work in Africa. All these government officials, who were part of the leadership in their respective governments, said they wanted us to send as many skilled people as we could contact. But this program never came into fruition, and we do not know the exact reasons, for I assure you that we talked and were committed to making this a successful program. It is our guess that the United States put the squeeze on these countries, for such a program directed by SNCC would have been too dangerous to the international prestige of the United States. It is also possible that some of the wild statements by some black leader frightened the Africans.

In Africa today there is a great suspicion of black people in this country. This is a correct suspicion since most of the Negroes who have left the States for work in Africa usually work for the Central Intelligence Agency (CIA) or the State Department. But the respect for us as a people continues to mount, and the day will come when we can return to our homeland as brothers and sisters. But we should not think of going back to Africa today, for we are located in a strategic position. We live inside the United States, which is the most barbaric country in the world, and we have a chance to help bring this government down.

Time is short, and we do not have much time, and it is time we stop mincing words. Caution is fine, but no oppressed people ever gained their liberation until they were ready to fight, to use whatever means necessary, including the use of force and power of the gun to bring down the colonizer.

We have heard the rhetoric, but we have not heard the rhetoric which says that black people in this country must understand that we are the vanguard force. We shall liberate all the people in the United States, and we will be instrumental in the liberation of colored people the world around. We must understand this point very clearly so that we are not trapped into diversionary and reactionary movements. Any class analysis of the United States shows very clearly that black people are the most oppressed group of people inside the United States. We have suffered the most from racism and exploitation, cultural degradation and lack of political power. It follows from the laws of revolution that the most oppressed will make the revolution, but we are not talking about just making the revolution. All the parties on the left who consider themselves revolutionary will say that blacks are the vanguard, but we are saying that not only are we the vanguard, but we must assume leadership, total control, and we must exercise the humanity which is inherent in us. We are the most humane people within the United States. We have suffered and we understand suffering. Our hearts go out to the Vietnamese, for we know what it is to suffer under the domination of racist America. Our hearts, our soul and all the compassion we can mount go out to our brothers in Africa, Santo Domingo, Latin America and Asia who are being tricked by the power structure of the United States which is dominating the world today. These ruthless, barbaric men have systematically tried to kill all people and organizations opposed to its imperialism. We no longer can just get by with the use of the word "capitalism" to describe the United States, for it is an imperial power sending money, missionaries and the Army throughout the world to protect this government and the few rich whites who control it. General Motors and all the major auto industries are operating in South Africa, yet the white-dominated leadership of the United Auto Workers sees no relationship to the exploitation of the black people in South Africa and the exploitation of black people in the United States. If they understand it, they certainly do not put it into practice, which is the actual test. We as black people must be concerned with the total conditions of all black people in the world.

But while we talk of revolution, which will be an armed confrontation and long years of sustained guerrilla warfare inside this country, we must also talk of the type of world we want to live in. We must commit ourselves to a society where the total means of production are taken from the rich and placed into the hands of the State for the welfare of all the people. This is what we mean when we say total control. And we mean that black people who have suffered the most from exploitation and racism must move to protect their black interest by assuming leadership inside of the United States of everything that exists. The time has ceased when we are second in command and the white boy stands on top. This is especially true of the welfare agencies in this country, but it is not enough to say that a black man is on top. He must be committed to building the new society, to taking the wealth away from the rich people, such as General Motors, Ford, Chrysler, the DuPonts, the Rockefellers, the Mellons, and all the other rich white exploiters and racists who run this world.

Where do we begin? We have already started. We started the moment we were brought to this country. In fact, we started on the shores of Africa, for we have always resisted attempts to make us slaves, and now we must resist the attempts to make us capitalist, for this will be the same line as that of integration into the mainstream of American life. Therefore, brothers and sisters, there is no need to fall into the trap that we have to get an ideology. We HAVE an ideology. Our fight is against racism, capitalism and imperialism, and we are dedicated to building a socialist society inside the United States where the total means of production and distribution are in the hands of the State, and that must be led by black people, by revolutionary blacks who are concerned about the total humanity of this world. And, therefore, we obviously are different from some of those who seek a black nation in the United States, for there is no way for that nation to be viable if in fact the United States remains in the hands of white racists. Then too, let us deal with some arguments that we should share power with whites. We say that there must be a revolutionary black vanguard, and that white people in this country must be willing to accept black leadership, for that is the only protection that black people have to protect ourselves from racism rising again in this country.

Racism in the United States is so pervasive in the mentality of whites, that only an armed, well-disciplined, black-controlled government can insure the stamping out of racism in this country. And that is why we plead with black people not to be talking about a few crumbs, a few thousand dollars for this cooperative, or a thousand dollars which splits black people into fighting over the dollar. That is the intention of the government. We say . . . think in terms of total control of the United States. Prepare ourselves to seize state power. Do not hedge, for time is short, and all around the world the forces of liberation are directing their attacks against the United States. It is a powerful country, but that power is not greater than that of black people. We work the chief industries in this country, and we would cripple the economy while the brothers fought guerrilla warfare in the streets. This will take some long-range planning, but whether it happens in a thousand years is of no consequence. It cannot happen unless we start. How then is all of this related to this conference?

First of all, this conference is called by a set of religious people, Christians, who have been involved in the exploitation and rape of black people since the country was founded. The missionary goes hand in hand with the power of the states. We must begin seizing power wherever we are, and we must say to the planners of this conference that you are no longer in charge. We the people who have assembled here thank you for getting us here, but we are going to assume power over the conference and determine from this moment on the direction in which we want it to go. We are not saying that the conference was planned badly. The staff of the conference has worked hard and has done a magnificent job in bringing all of us together, and we must include them in the new membership which must surface from this point on. The conference is now the property of the people who are assembled here. This we proclaim as fact and not rhetoric, and there are demands that we are going to make and we insist that the planners of this conference help us implement them.

We maintain we have the revolutionary right to do this. We have the same rights, if you will, as the Christians had in going into Africa and raping our Motherland and bringing us away from our continent of peace and into this hostile and alien environment where we have been living in perpetual warfare since 1619.

Our seizure of power at this conference is based on a program, and our program is contained in the following Manifesto:

Black Manifesto

We the black people assembled in Detroit, Michigan, for the National Black Economic Development Conference are fully aware that we have been forced to come together because racist white America has exploited our resources, our minds, our bodies, our labor. For centuries we have been forced to live as colonized people inside the United States, victimized by the most vicious, racist system in the world. We have helped to build the most industrialized country in the world.

We are therefore demanding of the white Christian churches and Jewish synagogues, which are part and parcel of the system of capitalism, that they begin to pay reparations to black people in this country. We are demanding $500,000,000 from the Christian white churches and the Jewish synagogues. This total comes to fifteen dollars per nigger. This is a low estimate, for we maintain there are probably more than 30,000,000 black people in this country. Fifteen dollars a nigger is not a large sum of money, and we know that the churches and synagogues have a tremendous wealth and its membership, white America, has profited and still exploits black people. We are also not unaware that the exploitation of colored peoples around the world is aided and abetted by the white Christian churches and synagogues. This demand for $500,000,000 is not an idle resolution or empty words. Fifteen dollars for every black brother and sister in the United States is only a beginning of the reparations due us as people who have been exploited and degraded, brutalized, killed and persecuted. Underneath all of this exploitation, the racism of this country has produced a psychological effect upon us that we are beginning to shake off. We are no longer afraid to demand our full rights as a people in this decadent society.

We are demanding $500,000,000 to be spent in the following way:
(1) We call for the establishment of a Southern land bank to help our brothers and sisters who have to leave their land because of racist pressure, and for people who want to establish cooperative farms but who have no funds. We have seen too many farmers evicted from their homes because they have dared to defy the white racism of this country. We need money for land. We must fight for massive sums of

money for this Southern land bank. We call for $200,000,000 to implement this program.

(2) We call for the establishment of four major publishing and printing industries in the United States to be funded with ten million dollars each. These publishing houses are to be located in Detroit, Atlanta, Los Angeles, and New York. They will help to generate capital for further cooperative investments in the black community, and provide jobs and an alternative to the white-dominated and controlled printing field.

(3) We call for the establishment of four of the most advanced scientific and futuristic audio-visual networks to be located in Detroit, Chicago, Cleveland and Washington, D.C. These TV networks will provide an alternative to the racist propaganda that fills the current television networks. Each of these TV networks will be funded by ten million dollars each.

(4) We call for a research skills center which will provide research on the problems of black people. This center must be funded with no less than thirty million dollars.

(5) We call for the establishment of a training center for the teaching of skills in community organization, photography, movie making, television making and repair, radio building and repair and all other skills needed in communication. This training center shall be funded with no less than ten million dollars.

(6) We recognize the role of the National Welfare Rights Organization, and we intend to work with them. We call for ten million dollars to assist in the organization of welfare recipients. We want to organize welfare workers in this country so that they may demand more money from the government and better administration of the welfare system of this country.

(7) We call for $20,000,000 to establish a National Black Labor Strike and Defense Fund. This is necessary for the protection of black workers and their families who are fighting racist working conditions in this country.

(8) We call for the establishment of the International Black Appeal (IBA). This International Black Appeal will be funded with no less than $20,000,000. The IBA is charged with producing more capital for the establishment of cooperative businesses in the United States and in Africa, our Motherland. The International Black Appeal is one of the most important demands that we are making, for we know

that it can generate and raise funds throughout the United States and help our African brothers. The IBA is charged with three functions and shall be headed by James Forman:

(a) Raising money for the program of the National Black Economic Development Conference.
(b) The development of cooperatives in African countries and support of African liberation movements.
(c) Establishment of a Black Anti-Defamation League which will protect our African image

(9) We call for the establishment of a black university to be founded with $130,000,000, to be located in the South. Negotiations are presently under way with a Southern university.

(10) We demand that IFCO allocate all unused funds in the planning budget to implement the demands of this conference.

In order to win our demands, we are aware that we will have to have massive support, therefore:

(1) We call upon all black people throughout the United States to consider themselves as members of the National Black Economic Development Conference and to act in unity to help force the racist white Christian churches and Jewish synagogues to implement these demands.

(2) We call upon all the concerned black people across the country to contact black workers, black women, black students and the black unemployed, community groups, welfare organizations, teachers' organizations, church leaders and organizations, explaining how these demands are vital to the black community of the United States. Pressure by whatever means necessary should be applied to the white power structure. All black people should act boldly in confronting our white oppressors and demanding this modest reparation of fifteen dollars per black man.

(3) Delegates and members of the National Black Economic Development Conference are urged to call press conferences in the cities and to attempt to get as many black organizations as possible to support the demands of the conference. The quick use of the press in the local areas will heighten the tension, and these demands must be attempted to be won in a short period of time, although we are prepared for protracted and long-range struggle.

(4) We call for the total disruption of selected church-sponsored agencies operating anywhere in the United States and the world. Black workers, black women, black students and the black unemployed are encouraged to seize the offices, telephones, and printing apparatus of all church-sponsored agencies and to hold these in trusteeship until our demands are met.

(5) We call upon all delegates and members of the National Black Economic Development Conference to stage sit-in demonstrations at selected black and white churches. This is not to be interpreted as a continuation of the sit-in movement of the early Sixties, but we know that active confrontation inside white churches is possible and will strengthen the possibility of meeting our demands. Such confrontation can take the form of reading the Black Manifesto instead of a sermon, or passing it out to church members. The principle of self-defense should be applied if attacked.

(6) On May 4, 1969, or a date thereafter, depending upon local conditions, we call upon black people to commence the disruption of the racist churches and synagogues throughout the United States.

(7) We call upon IFCO to serve as a central staff to coordinate the mandate of the conference and to reproduce and distribute en masse literature, leaflets, news items, press releases and other material.

(8) We call upon all delegates to find within the white community those forces which will work under the leadership of blacks to implement these demands by whatever means necessary. By taking such actions, white Americans will demonstrate concretely that they are willing to fight the white skin privilege and the white supremacy and racism which has forced us as black people to make these demands.

(9) We call upon all white Christians and Jews to practice patience, tolerance, understanding and nonviolence as they have encouraged, advised and demanded that we as black people should do throughout our entire enforced slavery in the United States. The true test of their faith and belief in the Cross and the words of the prophets will certainly be put to a test as we seek legitimate and extremely modest reparation for our role in developing the industrial base of the western world through our slave labor. But we are no longer slaves, we are men and women, proud of our African heritage, determined to have our dignity.

(10) We are so proud of our African heritage and realize concretely that our struggle is not only to make revolution in the United States

but to protect our brothers and sisters in Africa and to help them rid themselves of racism, capitalism and imperialism by whatever means necessary, including armed struggle. We are and must be willing to fight the defamation of our African image wherever it rears its ugly head. We are therefore charging the steering committee to create a black Anti-Defamation League to be founded by money raised from the International Black Appeal.

(11) We fully recognize that revolution in the United States and Africa, our Motherland, is more than a one-dimensional operation. It will require the total integration of the political, economic and military components, and therefore we call upon all our brothers and sisters who have acquired training and expertise in the fields of engineering, electronics, research, community organization, physics, biology, chemistry, mathematics, medicine, military science and warfare to assist the National Black Economic Development Conference in the implementation of its program.

(12) To implement these demands we must have a fearless leadership. We must have a leadership which is willing to battle the church establishment to implement these demands. To win our demands we will have to declare war on the white Christian churches and synagogues, and this means we may have to fight the total government structure of this country. Let no one here think that these demands will be met by our mere stating them. For the sake of the churches and synagogues, we hope that they have the wisdom to understand that these demands are modest and reasonable. But if the white Christians and Jews are not willing to meet our demands through peace and goodwill, then we declare war, and we are prepared to fight by whatever means necessary. We are, therefore, proposing the election of the following steering committee:

Lucius Walker	Mark Comfort
Renny Freeman	Earl Allen
Luke Tripp	Robert Browne
Howard Fuller	Vincent Harding
James Forman	Mike Hamlin
John Watson	Len Holt
Dan Aldridge	Peter Bernard
John Williams	Michael Wright

Ken Cockrel	Muhammed Kenyatta
Chuck Wooten	Mel Jackson
Fannie Lou Hamer	Howard Moore
Julian Bond	Harold Homes

Brothers and sisters, we are no longer shuffling our feet and scratching our heads. We are tall, black and proud.

And we say to the white Christian churches and Jewish synagogues, to the government of this country and to all the white racist imperialists who compose it, there is only one thing left that you can do to further degrade black people and that is to kill us. But we have been dying too long for this country. We have died in every war. We are dying in Vietnam today fighting the wrong enemy.

The new black man wants to live, and to live means that we must not become static or merely believe in self-defense. We must boldly go out and attack the white Western world at its power centers. The white Christian churches are another form of government in this country, and they are used by the government of this country to exploit the people of Latin America, Asia and Africa, but the day is soon coming to an end. Therefore, brothers and sisters, the demands we make upon the white Christian churches and the Jewish synagogues are small demands. They represent fifteen dollars per black person in these United States. We can legitimately demand this from the church power structure. We must demand more from the United States Government.

But to win our demands from the church, which is linked up with the United States Government, we must not forget that it will ultimately be by force and power that we will win.

We are not threatening the churches. We are saying that we know the churches came with the military might of the colonizers and have been sustained by the military might of the colonizers. Hence, if the churches in colonial territories were established by military might, we know deep within our hearts that we must be prepared to use force to get our demands. We are not saying that this is the road we want to take. It is not, but let us be very clear that we are not opposed to force and we are not opposed to violence. We were captured in Africa by violence. We were kept in bondage and political servitude and forced to work as slaves by the military machinery and the Christian Church working hand in hand.

We recognize that in issuing this Manifesto we must prepare for a long-range educational campaign in all communities of this country, but we know that the Christian churches have contributed to our oppression in white America. We do not intend to abuse our black brothers and sisters in black churches who have uncritically accepted Christianity. We want them to understand how the racist white Christian church with its hypocritical declarations and doctrines of brotherhood has abused our trust and faith. An attack on the religious beliefs of black people is not our major objective, even though we know that we were not Christians when we were brought to this country, but that Christianity was used to help enslave us. Our objective in issuing this Manifesto is to force the racist white Christian church to begin the payment of reparations which are due to all black people, not only by the church but also by private business and the United States Government. We see this focus on the Christian church as an effort around which all black people can unite.

Our demands are negotiable, but they cannot be minimized, they can only be increased, and the church is asked to come up with larger sums of money than we are asking. Our slogans are:

All Roads Must Lead to Revolution

Unite with Whomever You Can Unite

Neutralize Wherever Possible

Fight Our Enemies Relentlessly

Victory to the People

Life and Good Health to Mankind

Resistance to Domination by the White Christian
    Churches and the Jewish Synagogues

Revolutionary Black Power

We Shall Win Without a Doubt

C

*BLACK THEOLOGY: A STATEMENT OF THE NATIONAL COMMITTEE OF BLACK CHURCHMEN**

Why Black Theology?

Black people affirm their being. This affirmation is made in the whole experience of being black in the hostile American society. Black Theology is not a gift of the Christian gospel dispensed to slaves; rather it is an *appropriation* which black slaves made of the gospel given by their white oppressors. Black theology has been nurtured, sustained and passed on in the black churches in their various ways of expression. Black theology has dealt with all the ultimate and violent issues of life and death for a people despised and degraded.

The black church has not only nurtured black people but enabled them to survive brutalities that ought not to have been inflicted on any community of men. Black theology is the product of black Christian experience and reflection. It comes out of the past. It is strong in the present. And we believe it is redemptive for the future.

This indigenous theological formation of faith emerged from the stark need of the fragmented black community to affirm itself as a part of the Kingdom of God. White theology sustained the American slave system and negated the humanity of blacks. This indigenous black theology, based on the imaginative black experience, was the

* Produced by the Committee on Theological Prospectus, issued June 13, 1969, at the Interdenominational Theological Center, Atlanta, Georgia.

best hope for the survival of black people. This is a way of saying that black theology was already present in the spirituals and slave songs and exhortations of slave preachers and their descendants.

All theologies arise out of communal experience with God. At this moment in time, the black community seeks to express its theology in language that speaks to the contemporary mood of black people.

What Is Black Theology?

Black theology is a theology of black liberation. It seeks to plumb the black condition in the light of God's revelation in Jesus Christ, so that the black community can see that the gospel is commensurate with the achievement of black humanity. Black Theology is a theology of "blackness." It is the affirmation of black humanity that emancipates black people from white racism thus providing authentic freedom for both white and black people. It affirms the humanity of white people in that it says No to the encroachment of white oppression.

The message of liberation is the revelation of God as revealed in the incarnation of Jesus Christ. Freedom IS the gospel. Jesus is the Liberator! "He . . . hath sent me to preach deliverance to the captives" (Luke 4:18). Thus the black patriarchs and we ourselves know this reality despite all attempts of the white church to obscure it and to utilize Christianity as a means of enslaving blacks. The demand that Christ the Liberator imposes on all men *requires* all blacks to affirm their full dignity as persons and all whites to surrender their presumptions of superiority and abuses of power.

What Does This Mean?

It means that Black Theology must confront the issues which are a part of the reality of black oppression. We cannot ignore the powerlessness of the black community. Despite the *repeated requests* for significant programs of social change, the American people have refused to appropriate adequate sums of money for social reconstruction. White church bodies have often made promises only to follow with default. We must, therefore, once again call the attention of the nation and the church to the need for providing adequate resources of power (reparation).

Reparation is a part of the Gospel message. Zacheus knew well the necessity for repayment as an essential ingredient in repentance. "If I have taken anything from any man by false accusation, I restore him fourfold" (Luke 19:8). The church which calls itself the servant church must, like its Lord, be willing to strip itself of possessions in order to build and restore that which has been destroyed by the compromising bureaucrats and conscienceless rich. While reparation cannot remove the guilt created by the despicable deed of slavery, it is nonetheless, a positive response to the need for power in the black community. We are a people who have always related the value of the person to the possession of property, or the lack of it. Hence, the sharing or the restoration of wealth is a significant gesture toward the restoration of personhood.

What Is the Cost?

Living is risk. We take it in confidence. The black community has been brutalized and victimized over the centuries. The recognition that comes from seeing Jesus as Liberator and the Gospel as freedom empowers black men to risk themselves for freedom and for faith. This faith we affirm in the midst of a hostile, disbelieving society. We intend to exist by this faith at all times and in all places.

In spite of brutal deprivation and denial the black community has appropriated the spurious form of Christianity imposed upon it and made it into an instrument for resisting the extreme demands of oppression. It has enabled the black community to live through unfulfilled promises, unnecessary risks, and inhuman relationships.

As black theologians address themselves to the issues of the black revolution, it is incumbent upon them to say that the black community will not be turned from its course, but will seek complete fulfillment of the promises of the Gospel. Black people have survived the terror. We now commit ourselves to the risks of affirming the dignity of black personhood. We do this as men and as black Christians. This is the message of Black Theology. In the words of Eldridge Cleaver,

We shall have our manhood. We shall have it or the earth will be leveled by our efforts to gain it.

D

*THE BLACK PAPER**

I. Our Confession

We, a group of black Methodists in America, are deeply disturbed about the crisis of racism in America. We are equally concerned about the failure of a number of black people, including black Methodists, to respond appropriately to the roots and forces of racism and the current Black Revolution.

We, as black Methodists, must first respond in a state of confession because it is only as we confront ourselves that we are able to deal with the evils and forces which seek to deny our humanity.

We confess our failure to be reconciled with ourselves as black men. We have too often denied our blackness (hair texture, color and other God-given physical characteristics) rather than embrace it in all its black beauty.

We confess that we have not always been relevant in service and ministry to our black brothers, and in so doing we have alienated ourselves from many of them.

We confess that we have not always been honest with ourselves and with our white brothers. We have not encountered them with truth but often with deception. We have not said in bold language and forceful action that, "You have used 'white power' in and outside of

* A statement (in part) of the findings of the Black Methodists for Church Renewal (in conference at Cincinnati, Ohio, February 6-9, 1968).

the church to keep us in a subordinate position." We have failed to tell our white brothers "like it is!" Instead, we have told our white brothers what we thought they would like to hear.

We confess that we have not become significantly involved in the Black Revolution because, for the most part, white men have defined it as "bad"; for the other part, we have been too comfortable in our "little world," and too pleased with our lot as second-class citizens and second-class members of The Methodist Church.

We confess that we have accepted too long the philosophy of racism. This has created a relationship in which white people have always defined the "terms," and, in fact, defined when and how black people would exist.

We confess that we have accepted a "false kind of integration" in which all power remained in the hands of white men.

II. The Black Revolution

"The Black Revolution is a fact! It is a call for black people throughout the nation and the world to stand on their feet and declare their independence from white domination and exploitation. The mood of the day is for black people to throw off the crippling myths of white superiority and black inferiority. The old myths are being replaced by black pride, self-development, self-awareness, self-respect, self-determination and black solidarity." * We are new men—the old man, "nigger," is dead! The "boy" is now a man!

We now stand as proud black men prepared to embrace our blackness and committed to address ourselves unequivocally and forcefully to racism wherever we find it, in and outside the church.

III. Black Power

How then do we respond forcefully and responsibly to racism in America and racism in The United Methodist Church? We unashamedly reply—Black Power!

* Archie Rich, "The Black Methodist's Response to Black Power" (a mimeographed paper prepared for the National Conference of Negro Methodists, Cincinnati, Ohio, February 6–9, 1968).

"It is abundantly clear to many Americans that power is basic to all human dynamics. The fundamental distortion facing us in a controversy about 'black power' is rooted in a gross imbalance of power and conscience between Negroes and white Americans. It is this distortion, mainly, which is responsible for the widespread, though often inarticulate, assumption that white people are justified in getting what they want through the use of power, but that Negro Americans must, either by nature or by circumstance, make their appeal only through conscience. As a result, the power of white men and the conscience of black men have both been corrupted." *

Black power provides the means by which black people do for themselves that which no other group can do for them.

" . . . Black power speaks to the need for black people to move from the stance of humble, dependent and impotent beggars to the stature of men who will take again into their own hands, as all men must, the fashioning of their own destiny for their own growth into self-development and self-respect. **

Black power is a call for black people in this country to unite, to recognize their heritage, and to build a sense of community. It is a call for us to take the initiative, to build the kind of community which crosses all class lines and geographical lines, in order that the resources and leadership of all black people may be used.

Black power means the development and utilization of the gifts of black men for the good of black men and the whole nation.

Finally, it is a call for us to respond to God's action in history which is to make and keep human life human.

* "Statement of Black Power" (a mimeographed paper developed by the National Committee of Negro Churchmen, July 31, 1966).
** Nathan Wright, Jr., *Black Power and Urban Unrest* (New York: Hawthorne Books, 1967), p. 60.

E

*WHAT THE MUSLIMS BELIEVE**

1. WE BELIEVE in the One God Whose proper Name is Allah.

2. WE BELIEVE in the Holy Qur-an and in the Scriptures of all the Prophets of God.

3. WE BELIEVE in the truth of the Bible, but we believe that it has been tampered with and must be reinterpreted so that mankind will not be snared by the falsehoods that have been added to it.

4. WE BELIEVE in Allah's Prophets and Scriptures they brought to the people.

5. WE BELIEVE in the resurrection of the dead—not in physical resurrection—but in mental resurrection. We believe that the so-called Negroes are most in need of mental resurrection: therefore, they will be resurrected first.

Furthermore, we believe we are the people of God's choice, as it has been written, that God would choose the rejected and the despised. We can find no other persons fitting this description in these last days more than the so-called Negroes in America. We believe in the resurrection of the righteous.

* *Muhammad Speaks* (July 13, 1973).

6. WE BELIEVE in the judgment; we believe this first judgment will take place as God revealed, in America . . . .

7. WE BELIEVE this is the time in history for the separation of the so-called white Americans. We believe the black man should be freed in name as well as in fact. By this we mean that he should be freed from the names imposed upon him by his former slave masters. Names which identified him as being the slave master's slave. We believe that if we are free indeed, we should go in our own people's names—the black peoples of the earth.

8. WE BELIEVE in justice for all, whether in God or not; we believe as others, that we are due equal justice as human beings. We believe in equality—as a nation—of equals. We do not believe that we are equal with our slave masters in the status of "freed slaves."

We recognize and respect American citizens as independent peoples and we respect their laws which govern this nation.

9. WE BELIEVE that the offer of integration is hypocritical and is made by those who are trying to deceive the black peoples into believing that their 400-year-old open enemies of freedom, justice and equality are, all of a sudden, their "friends." Furthermore, we believe that such deception is intended to prevent black people from realizing that the time in history has arrived for the separation from the whites of this nation.

If the white people are truthful about their professed friendship toward the so-called Negro, they can prove it by dividing up America with their slaves.

We do not believe that America will ever be able to furnish enough jobs for her own millions of unemployed, in addition to jobs for the 20,000,000 black people as well.

10. WE BELIEVE that we who declared ourselves to be righteous Muslims, should not participate in wars which take the lives of humans. We do not believe this nation should force us to take part in such wars, for we have nothing to gain from it unless America agrees to give us the necessary territory wherein we may have something to fight for.

11. WE BELIEVE our women should be respected and protected as the women of other nationalities are respected and protected.

12. WE BELIEVE that Allah (God) appeared in the Person of Master W. Fard Muhammad, July, 1930; the long-awaited "Messiah" of the Christians and the "Mahdi" of the Muslims.

We believe further and lastly that Allah is God and besides HIM there is no God and He will bring about a universal government of peace wherein we all can live in peace together.

F

WHAT THE MUSLIMS WANT*

This is the question asked most frequently by both the whites and the blacks. The answers to this question I shall state as simply as possible.

1. We want freedom. We want a full and complete freedom.

2. We want justice. Equal justice under the law. We want justice applied equally to all, regardless of creed or class or color.

3. We want equality of opportunity. We want equal membership in society with the best in civilized society.

4. We want our people in America whose parents or grandparents were descendants from slaves, to be allowed to establish a separate state or territory of their own—either on this continent or elsewhere. We believe that our former slave masters are obligated to provide such land and that the area must be fertile and minerally rich. We believe that our former slave masters are obligated to maintain and supply our needs in this separate territory for the next 20 to 25 years—until we are able to produce and supply our own needs.

Since we cannot get along with them in peace and equality, after giving them 400 years of our sweat and blood and receiving in return

* *Muhammad Speaks* (July 13, 1973).

some of the worst treatment human beings have ever experienced, we believe our contributions to this land and the suffering forced upon us by white America, justify our demand for complete separation in a state or territory of our own.

5. We want freedom for all Believers of Islam now held in Federal prisons. We want freedom for all black men and women now under death sentence in innumerable prisons in the North as well as the South.

We want every black man and woman to have the freedom to accept or reject being separated from the slave master's children and establish a land of their own.

We know that the above plan for the solution of the black and white conflict is the best and only answer to the problem between two people.

6. We want an immediate end to the police brutality and mob attacks against the so-called Negro throughout the United States.

We believe that the Federal government should intercede to see that black men and women tried in white courts receive justice in accordance with the laws of the land—or allow us to build a new nation for ourselves, dedicated to justice, freedom and liberty.

7. As long as we are not allowed to establish a state or territory of our own, we demand not only equal justice under the laws of the United States, but equal employment opportunities—NOW!

We do not believe that after 400 years of free or nearly free labor, sweat and blood, which has helped America become rich and powerful, that so many thousands of black people should have to subsist on relief, charity or live in poor houses.

8. We want the government of the United States to exempt our people from ALL taxation as long as we are deprived of equal justice under the laws of the land.

9. We want equal education—but separate schools up to 16 for boys and 18 for girls on the condition that the girls be sent to women's colleges and universities. We want all black children educated, taught and trained by their own teachers.

Under such schooling system we believe we will make a better nation of people. The United States government should provide, free, all necessary textbooks and equipment, schools and college buildings. The Muslim teachers shall be left free to teach and train their people in the way of righteousness, decency and self-respect.

10. We believe that intermarriage or race mixing should be prohibited. We want the religion of Islam taught without hindrance or suppression.

These are some of the things that we, the Muslims, want for our people in North America.

NOTES

Chapter 1: Introduction

1. E. Franklin Frazier, *The Negro Church in America*, p. 8.
2. See Frazier, pp. 23–25.
3. Charles H. Wesley, *Richard Allen, Apostle of Freedom* (Washington, D. C., 1935), pp. 15–17.
4. L. D. Reddick, *Crusader Without Violence* (New York, 1959). See Chaps. VIII and IX, pp. 108–45.
5. *Op. cit.*, pp. 183ff.

Chapter 2: The Power in the Black Church

1. Now the United Church of Christ.
2. Now the United Methodist Church.
3. Woodstock College in Maryland.
4. Yale University and Union Theological Seminary in New York. Union, with the strong backing of Columbia University, won, and Woodstock moved to Morningside Heights in 1970.
5. The Protestant Episcopal Church, the Disciples of Christ, the Presbyterian Church (USA), the United Presbyterian Church, the United Methodist Church, the United Church of Christ, and three Black denominations—the African Methodist Episcopal Church, the African Methodist Episcopal Church, Zion, and the Christian Methodist Episcopal Church.
6. The Presbyterians later reaffiliated.

7. See note 5. These three denominations had a combined membership of about 2.5 million in 1966.

8. National Baptist Convention USA, 5,500,000 members; National Baptist Convention of America, 2,668,000 members; Progressive Baptist Convention, Inc., 505,000 members. All figures are for 1966.

9. Lerone Bennett, *What Manner of Man* (Chicago, 1968), p. 80.

10. *Ibid.*, p. 65.

11. *Ibid.*, p. 66.

12. *Ibid.*, p. 82.

13. David Lewis, *King* (New York, 1970), p. 89.

14. *Ibid.*, p. 158.

15. Executive Director of SCLC 1960–64.

16. Head of the SCLC affiliate in Alabama.

17. Close associate of Dr. King's and his successor as president of SCLC.

18. Founder of OIC (Opportunity Industrialization Centers) in Philadelphia and other cities. OIC provides training, skills, and placement for the "hard-core unemployed" of America's slums.

19. Leon H. Sullivan, *Build Brother Build* (Philadelphia, 1969), p. 70.

20. *Ibid.*, p. 67.

21. June 24, 1962.

22. Sullivan, *op. cit.,* pp. 85ff.

23. *Ibid.*, pp. 77ff.

24. See notes 5 and 8. See also Charles V. Hamilton, *The Black Preacher in America* (New York, 1972), pp. 70ff., for a breakdown of membership in the lesser Black communions.

25. Gayraud Wilmore, Jr., *Black Religion and Black Radicalism* (New York, 1972), pp. 247ff. The term seems to have originated with Adam Clayton Powell, who in an address at Howard University on May 29, 1966, declared that "Human rights are God given . . . to demand these God-given rights is to seek black power, the power to build black institutions . . . ." See Floyd B. Barbaus, *The Black Power Revolt* (Boston, 1968), p. 189; C. Nathan Wright, Jr., *Black Power and Urban Unrest* (New York, 1967), p. 13.

26. Nathan Wright, *op. cit.,* cover flap.

27. *Ibid.*

28. *Ibid.*

29. Martin Luther King, *"Where Do We Go from Here: Chaos or Community?"* (New York, 1967), p. 30.

30. Wright, *op. cit.,* pp.2–3.

31. Wilmore, *op. cit.,* p. 248.

32. Congress of Racial Equality. Organized in 1942 for "non-violent direct action" in civil rights. It was the first group to use the "sit-in" as a direct-action technique.

33. For a more complete treatment of the Black Muslims, see Chapter 4.

34. Then Secretary of the Commission on Religion and Race, The National Council of Churches.

35. Wilmore, *op. cit.*, p. 267.

36. July 31, 1966.

37. See Appendix A for the entire text of the statement and the list of signatories thereto.

38. November 1967.

39. For a detailed discussion of NCBC, IFCO, and the Black Economic Development Conference, see Wilmore, *op. cit.*, pp. 274ff.

40. The person or persons who drafted the body of the statement were not identified. The preamble was James Forman's personal statement. There was disagreement as to whether the manifesto was properly introduced before the house, and many of the six hundred delegates abstained from voting. Rev. Lucius Walker, president of IFCO, announced that the vote for approval was 187 to 63. There was no action taken to rescind the vote.

41. See Appendix B for full text of the manifesto.

42. Arnold Schuster, *Reparations* (Philadelphia, 1970), p. 6.

43. *Ibid.*

44. An excellent catalogue and analysis of white Church response appear in Robert S. Lecky and H. Elliott Wright, *Black Manifesto* (New York, 1969), pp. 16ff.

45. *Ibid.*

46. Prominent black sociologist and lay churchman.

47. Schuster, *op. cit.*, p. 14.

Chapter 3: The New Black Theology

1. William Hordern, *A Layman's Guide to Protestant Theology* (New York, 1955), pp. 3–4.

2. Vergilius Ferm, "Theology," in *Encyclopedia of Religion* (New York, 1945).

3. David Wesley Soper, *Major Voices in American Theology* (Philadelphia, 1953), p. 10.

4. Hordern, *op. cit.*, p. 6.

5. Edwin Lewis, *Jesus Christ and the Human Quest* (New York, 1924), p. 38.

6. *Beyond Tragedy* (New York, 1938), p. 96.

7. *Op. cit.*, p. 31.

8. Preston Williams, "The Black Church: Origin, History and Present Dilemmas" (unpublished), pp. 15–16.

9. Adam Clayton Powell, *Keep the Faith, Baby!* (New York, 1967), p. 233.

10. Reuben Sheares II, "Beyond White Theology," *Christianity and Crisis*, November 2, 1970, p. 229.

11. Preston Williams, "Ethos and Ethics" (unpublished), p. 5.

12. *The Atlanta University Publications* (New York, 1968), p. 29.

13. *A Black Theology of Liberation* (New York, 1970), p. 31.

14. Professor Hordern being the sole exception, for though a Canadian by birth, he has spent much of his professional life working and teaching in America.

15. *Op. cit.*, p. 7.

16. Williams, "The Black Church," pp. 15–16.

17. *Op. cit.*, pp. 11–12.

18. *Black Theology and Black Power* (New York, 1969), p. 120.

19. Lawrence Jones, "Fresh Perspectives on the Theology of the Invisible Institution, 1619–1860," *Union Quarterly Review,* Spring 1973.

20. Quoted in John Bracey, *et al., Black Nationalism in America* (New York, 1970), pp. 154–55.

21 *Ibid.*, p. 155.

22. See C. Eric Lincoln, *The Black Muslims in America*, rev. edn. (Boston, 1973).

23. See, for example, Bernard Cushmeer's *This Is the One*, an extraordinary polemic on Elijah Muhammad (Phoenix, Ariz. 1970).

Chapter 4: The Nation of Islam

1. See Winthrop D. Jordan, *White Over Black* (Chapel Hill, N. C., 1968), p. 183.

2. For a detailed account of the Muslim kingdoms of West Africa, see Basil Davidson, *A History of West Africa* (New York, 1966). See also John S. Mbiti, *African Religions and Philosophy* (New York, 1967).

3. See C. Eric Lincoln, *The Black Muslims in America*, rev. edn. (Boston, 1973), p. 12.

4. *Ibid.,* p. 90.

5. Thomas F. Gossett, *Race: The History of an Idea in America* (New York, 1965), p. 293.

6. Fitzgerald translation.

7. Lincoln, *op. cit.,* p. 28.

SELECTED
BIBLIOGRAPHY

Barrett, Leonard. *Soul Force: African Heritage in Afro-American Religion.* New York: Doubleday, forthcoming 1974.

Bennett, Lerone. *What Manner of Man.* New York: Pocket Books, 1968.

Carmichael, Stokely, and Hamilton, Charles V. *Black Power: The Politics of Liberation in America.* New York: Random House, 1968.

Cleage, Albert. *The Black Messiah.* New York: Sheed and Ward, 1968.

Cone, James H. *A Black Theology of Liberation.* New York: Lippincott, 1970.

Cushmeer, Bernard. *This Is the One.* Phoenix, Ariz.: Truth Publications, 1970.

Haley, Alex, ed. *The Autobiography of Malcolm X.* New York: Grove Press, 1965.

Hamilton, Charles V. *The Black Preacher in America.* New York: William Morrow, 1972.

Hough, Joseph, Jr. *Black Power and White Protestants.* New York: Oxford University Press, 1968.

Jones, William. *Is God a White Racist?* New York: Doubleday, 1973.

Jordan, Winthrop D. *White over Black.* Chapel Hill, N. C.: University of North Carolina Press, 1968.

Lewis, David L. *King, A Critical Biography.* Baltimore, Md.: Penguin, 1971.

Lincoln, C. Eric. *The Black Muslims in America.* Rev. edn. Boston: Beacon, 1973.

———*My Face Is Black.* Boston: Beacon, 1964.

———*The Negro Pilgrimage in America.* New York: Bantam Books, 1967.

Mitchell, Henry H. *Black Preaching.* New York: Lippincott, 1970.

Reddick, L. D. *Crusader Without Violence.* New York: Harper & Row, 1959.

Roberts, J. Deotis. *Liberation and Reconciliation: A Black Theology.* Philadelphia: Westminster, 1971.

Skinner, Tom. *How Black Is the Gospel?* New York: Lippincott, 1970.

Washington, Joseph R., Jr. *Black Religion: The Negro and Christianity in the United States.* Boston: Beacon, 1964.

———*Black Sects and Cults.* New York: Doubleday, 1973.

Wilmore, Gayraud, Jr. *Black Religion and Black Radicalism.* New York: Doubleday, 1972.

INDEX TO NEGRO CHURCH IN AMERICA

INDEX TO THE BLACK CHURCH SINCE FRAZIER